cooking WITH curious chef®

Get Kids Really Cooking with Step by Step Recipes and Activities

BARBARA J. BRANDT, M.ED.

THIS BOOK BELONGS TO:

TAILORMADE products

Get Kids Really Cooking
WITH REAL KITCHEN TOOLS

NOTE: The recipes in this book are intended for children 4 years and up together with a supervising adult. It is assumed that the supervising adult will use their own judgment and common sense to determine how much supervision the young chef needs and whether or not he or she is capable of performing the tasks required to complete each recipe. Neither the author nor the publisher nor the manufacturer assume any responsibility or liability for any injuries or damages arising during the preparation of the recipes or activities contained herein.

Author	Barbara J. Brandt, M.Ed.
Editing	Tailor Made Products, Inc.
Managing Editor	Prowrite Consulting and Editing
Interior Design	rosa+wesley, inc.
Art Editor	Mekael Wesley-Rosa
Photography	Tailor Made Products, Inc. and Rachael Smith

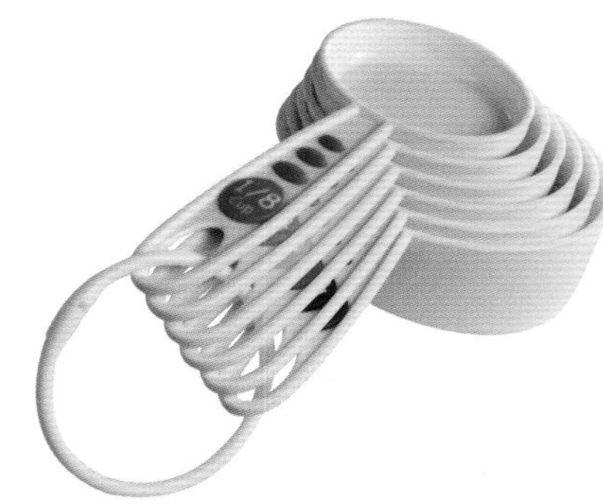

Published by Tailor Made Products, Inc.
101 Juneau Street
Elroy, WI 53929

Printed in Malaysia

First Edition
ISBN: 978-0-692-59913-6

This product is available at quantity discounts for bulk purchases. For more information, please contact Tailor Made Products, Inc. at sales@curiouschef.com or 1(800) 932-8227.

Table of Contents

Getting Started 4
Cooking with Kids 5
About Curious Chef 6
Note to Grown Ups 8
Chapter Sneak Peek 9
Kitchen Safety 12

Cupcake & Decorating Kit
- Oatmeal Carrot Muffins 14
- Vanilla Cupcakes 22
- Egg and Cheese Breakfast Bites 23

Pizza Kit
- Fruit Pizza 26
- Breakfast Pizza 34
- Taco Pizza 35

Pie Kit
- Banana Cream Pie 38
- Chicken Pot Pie 46
- Cherry Pie 47

Fruit & Veggie Prep Kit
- Apple Pie Cake 50
- Chicken Melon Salad 58
- Potato Pancakes 59

Cookie Kit
- Peanut Butter Whoopie Cookies 62
- Fruit Pocket Cookies 70
- Double Chocolate Dream Cookies 71

Measure & Prep Kit
- Italian Meatballs 74
- Cranberry Granola Bars 82
- Blueberry Croissant Puff 83

Pink Chef's Kit
- French Toast Pops 86
- Basic White Bread 94
- Welsh Cakes 95

Blue Chef's Kit
- Chocolate Zucchini Muffins 98
- Beef Stir Fry 106
- Raspberry Scones 107

Yellow Chef's Kit
- Sausage and Potato Frittata 110
- Banana Bread 118
- Breakfast Crepes 119

Cookie Cutter Collection
- Ice Cream Sandwich Cookies 122
- Raspberry Bark 130
- Fruit Tart Hearts 131

Foundation Set
- Baked Peaches 'n Cream 134
- Chocolate Custard Tarts 142
- Parmesan Cheddar Crackers 143

Caddy Collection
- Quiche Lorraine 146
- Fruit Salsa and Chips 154
- Chicken Quesadillas 155

Have Some Fun! Activity Solutions 158

Getting Started

Because of our new and innovative approach to introducing kids to cooking, it will be helpful to familiarize yourself with our unique and kid-friendly recipe format and the features in each chapter that make learning to cook with Curious Chef® so successful. So before you embark on this cooking adventure, take a few minutes to review the following important information in this section.

Why Get Your Kids Cooking with Curious Chef?

Summary of the added benefits that lie in store for you and your child when you bring them into your kitchen to cook with you.

Curious Chef Product Information

Learn about Curious Chef products and how they help inspire a life-long love of cooking in children.

Note to Grown Ups

Tips and suggestions for how to guide, support and help your young sous chef as you work together in the kitchen.

Chapter Sneak Peek

Overview of our unique, kid-friendly recipe format, along with a sneak peek of all the important features and fun activities found in each chapter that make this book one of a kind.

Kitchen Safety

Important safety guidelines to review with your child to make sure the cooking experience is a safe one.

Cooking With Kids

At Curious Chef, we believe that teaching children to cook helps build a foundation for many essential life skills. And when you get Cooking with Curious Chef, we make it more than just fun and easy. You and your child will also enjoy a whole host of additional benefits, including:

1 **Your child will be empowered to eat healthier.** In addition to learning basic cooking skills, kids also learn the basics of nutrition and how to make healthy food choices. The more kids understand about how to build a healthy plate, the easier it is for them to make healthy food choices—now and in the future.

2 **You will spend quality time with your child.** Cooking with Curious Chef is designed specifically to bring kids and parents together in the kitchen so you can spend quality time with your child while at the same time they learn a valuable lifelong skill.

3 **Your child will be more willing to try new foods.** Studies have shown that when kids take part in the preparation of food they are much more likely to not just try new foods, but also to like foods that they otherwise think they don't. Bringing kids into the kitchen increases the variety and types of foods they will eat.

4 **Your child will develop self-esteem and confidence.** Taking on the challenge and responsibility for learning to cook and mastering new skills is a surefire way to boost confidence and build self-esteem. Imagine your child beaming with pride as they share the food they made with friends and family!

5 **You'll create memories that will last a lifetime.** Laughing, talking, sharing, having fun! This is just some of what's in store for you and your child when you're in the kitchen together enjoying each other's company. Cooking with Curious Chef provides a unique opportunity for you to create special moments with your child that you will cherish forever.

6 **Your child will develop other essential skills.** When kids get busy in the kitchen, they are developing math skills, watching science in action, strengthening listening and organizational skills and learning to follow directions. There's nothing like hands-on learning to bring what they learn in school to life!

About Curious Chef

Curious Chef is all about creating fun family memories, and what better place to make those memories than in the kitchen? Kids are starting to cook at a younger age than ever before, and Curious Chef is proud to provide these young aspiring chefs with the tools they need to have fun, stay safe and get creative in the process.

All our tools are designed with small hands in mind, meaning they are safer than traditional cooking tools, have softer easy-grip handles and sturdier bases, larger numbers with corresponding colors for easy-to-learn measuring, and are better equipped to handle the types of spills and slips that can often happen when kids are cooking. And, because they're fully functional cooking tools,

16 PIECE – **Cupcake & Decorating Kit**

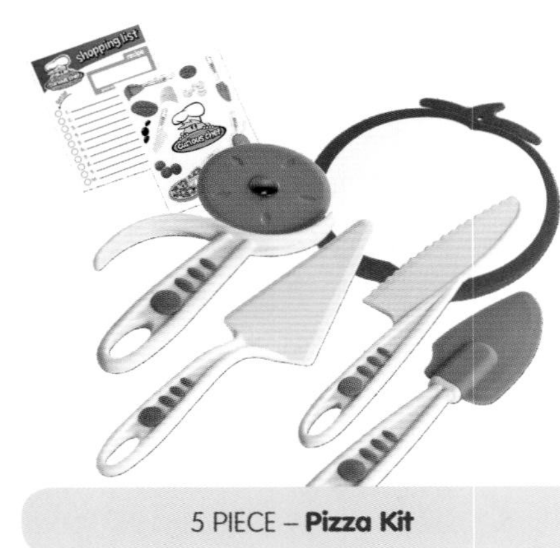

5 PIECE – **Pizza Kit**

5 PIECE – **Pie Kit**

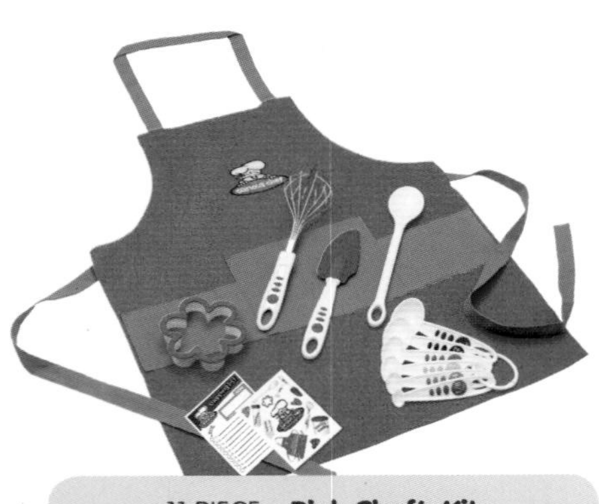

11 PIECE – **Pink Chef's Kit**

11 PIECE – **Blue Chef's Kit**

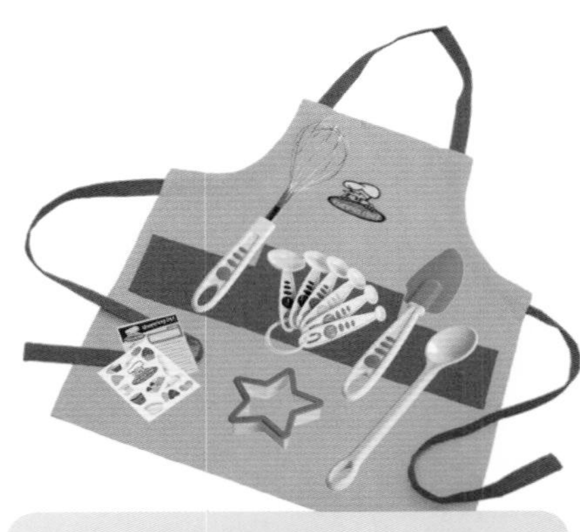

11 PIECE – **Yellow Chef's Kit**

young chefs can join in alongside their adult helper and help out with all stages of the recipe preparation, whether it be creating a special French toast breakfast, savory Parmesan cheddar crackers, or a spaghetti and meatball dinner for the whole family. With Curious Chef tools, anything is possible!

The recipes in each chapter focus on the tools found in each of the 12 kits shown below. And while you do not need the kits to complete the recipes, cooking with Curious Chef tools makes it easier and more fun for kids to complete the recipes on their own.

Find these great kits and many others on CuriousChef.com

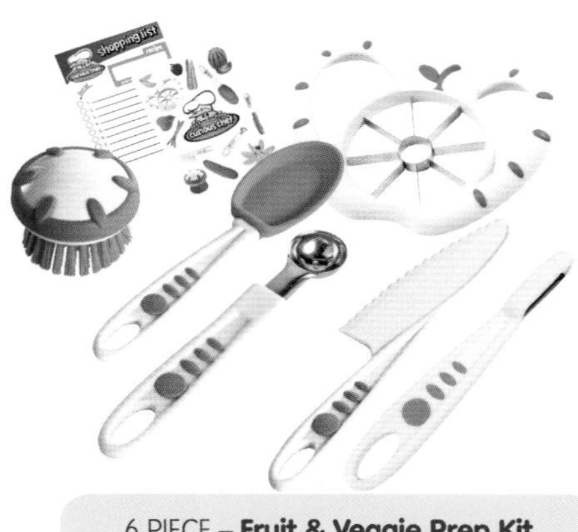

6 PIECE – **Fruit & Veggie Prep Kit**

6 PIECE – **Cookie Kit**

17 PIECE – **Measure & Prep Kit**

16 PIECE – **Cookie Cutter Collection**

27 PIECE – **Foundation Set**

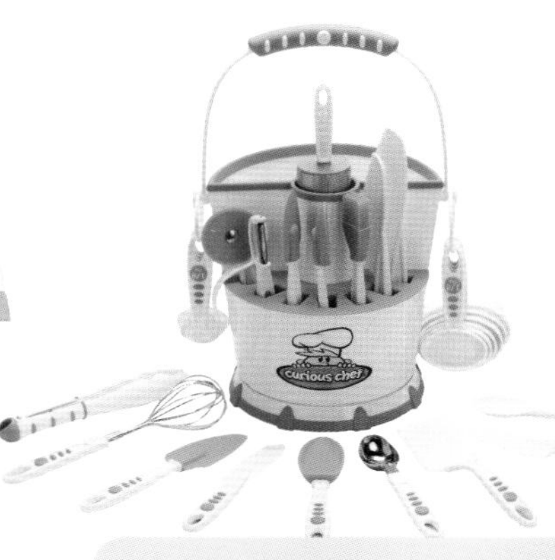

30 PIECE – **Caddy Collection**

Note to Grown Ups

Although bringing your kids into the kitchen to help you cook is extremely rewarding, it is not without its challenges. Messes will be made, things may get broken, and mistakes will be made. When cooking with Curious Chef, we want your experience to be a great one, so we offer a few suggestions that will help to make your time in the kitchen with your young chef as enjoyable and successful as possible.

Have Fun!

Cooking should be fun, not a chore. Embrace the experience with a spirit of adventure and a joy for learning. It's all about the journey, not the destination, so have fun, relax, and enjoy every step along the way.

View Mistakes as Opportunities to Learn

Things are bound to go wrong once in a while, but that's just part of the learning process. When mistakes happen, try to view them as opportunities to learn and improve so they can do better the next time.

Reflect on the Learning Experience

Talking about an experience is a great way to learn more from it. Discuss what went right and laugh about what went wrong. Talk about what you might do differently next time and reflect on all the positive things that came out of the experience.

Clean As You Go

To keep after-meal clean up to a minimum, prepare some soapy dishwater before you start cooking. When you're waiting for things to heat up or cool down, use this time to wash a few dishes and there will be little left to do when you're done cooking.

Be Supportive Without Taking Over

Kids can and will rise to meet any appropriate challenge—if we let them! Unless it's a matter of your child's safety, try to offer help only when asked for it. Kids learn by doing, and the more they do, the more they learn and take pride in their accomplishments.

Chapter Sneak Peek

Check here to find out how long it takes to prepare the recipe and how long until it's time to dig in and enjoy!

Chefs-in-Training
Check here to see what new skills your young chef will learn by making the recipes in the chapter.

ChooseMyPlate.gov
Young chefs learn how the ingredients used in the recipe fit into the five food groups that make up a healthy and balanced meal.

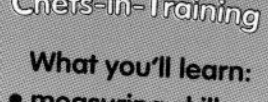

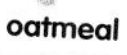

Chefs-in-Training
What you'll learn:
- measuring skills
- baking
- whisking
- cracking eggs
- melting chocolate

Shopping List
Got it!
- quick cooking oatmeal (1 ½ cups)
- peanut butter (1 ½ cups)
- egg (1)
- flour (½ cup)
- sugar (½ cup)
- butter (½ cup)
- brown sugar (½ cup)
- powdered sugar (½ cup)
- baking powder (½ tsp)
- baking soda (½ tsp)
- salt (½ tsp)
- vanilla extract (½ tsp)
- baking chocolate (6 oz)

Note to Grown Ups
The Curious Chef Cookie Kit comes with all the tools your sous chef needs to make the cookie dough, but you will need a double-boiler to melt the chocolate coating for the cookies. If you don't own a double boiler you can easily make your own by placing a metal or glass bowl over a large saucepan.

62

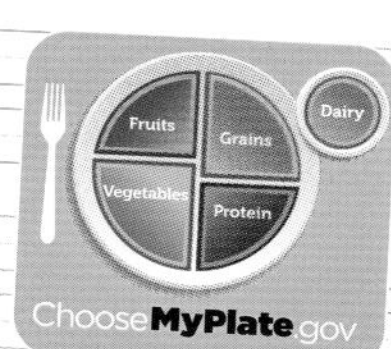

What's On Your Plate?
Write the ingredients that are part of a healthy plate where they belong on the organizer.

oatmeal
butter
Fruits
Grains
Dairy
Vegetables
Protein
ChooseMyPlate.gov
peanut butter

Cross out the ingredients that are not part of a healthy plate.

peanut butter
flour
sugar

Cookie Kit

Which ingredient is a whole-grain?

Which ingredient is both a source of protein and high in fat calories?

Food Facts
What do chocolate and coffee have in common?
More than you might think. Chocolate is made from cocoa beans which grow on the cacao tree. They look very much like coffee beans and are roasted much the same way. After roasting, the shells are removed and what's left is cocoa butter and chocolate solids, which are then turned into the final product we call chocolate.

63

Note to Grown Ups
Check here for select information about the tools used and tips for successfully completing the recipe.

Check here for questions designed to test your young chef's knowledge of the ingredients used in the recipe.

Food Facts
Check here for additional nutritional information about select ingredients.

Shopping List
Check here to make sure you have everything you need before you start cooking.

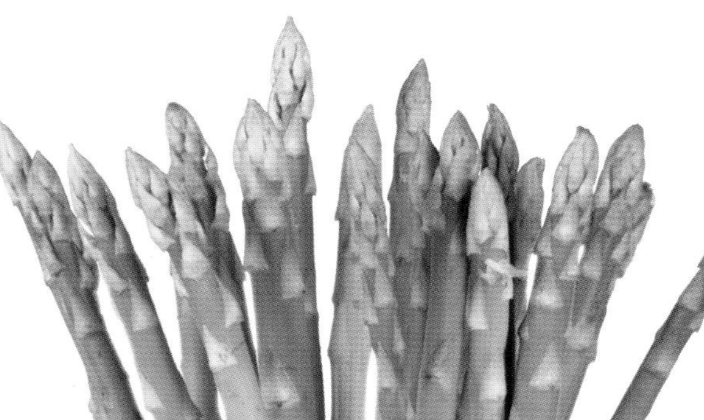

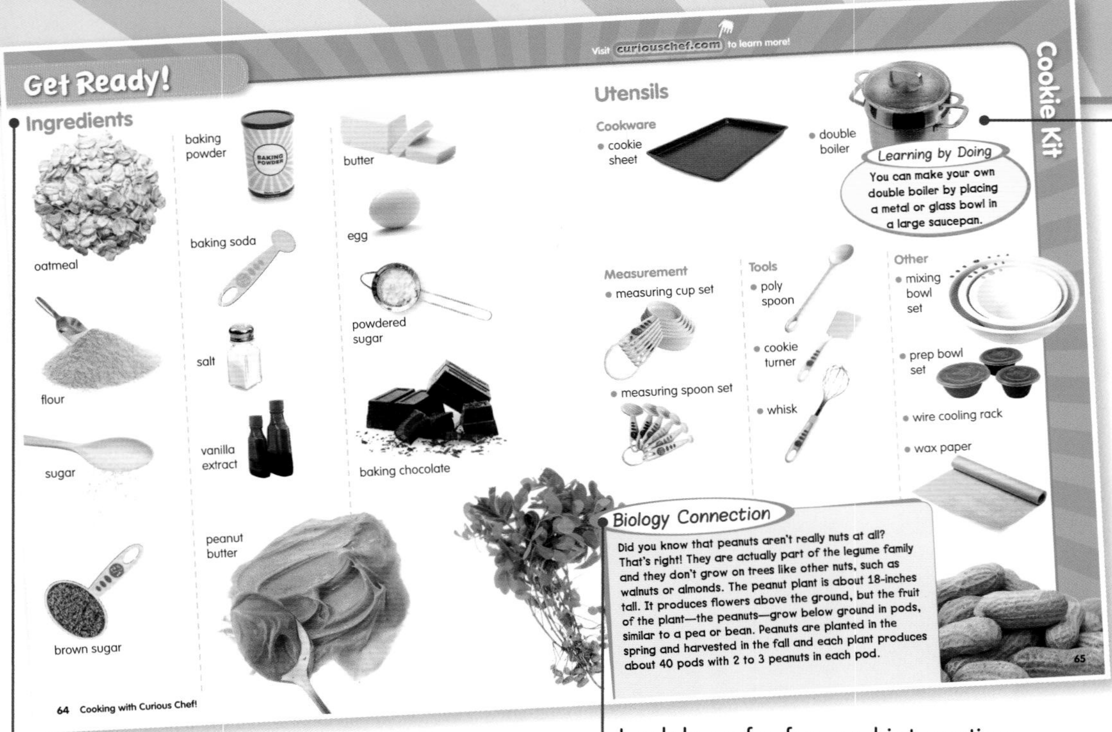

Visit curiouschef.com to learn more!

Get Ready!

Ingredients

oatmeal
flour
sugar
brown sugar
baking powder
baking soda
salt
vanilla extract
peanut butter
butter
egg
powdered sugar
baking chocolate

Utensils

Cookware
- cookie sheet
- double boiler

Learning by Doing
You can make your own double boiler by placing a metal or glass bowl in a large saucepan.

Measurement
- measuring cup set
- measuring spoon set

Tools
- poly spoon
- cookie turner
- whisk

Other
- mixing bowl set
- prep bowl set
- wire cooling rack
- wax paper

Biology Connection
Did you know that peanuts aren't really nuts at all? That's right! They are actually part of the legume family and they don't grow on trees like other nuts, such as walnuts or almonds. The peanut plant is about 18-inches tall. It produces flowers above the ground, but the fruit of the plant—the peanuts—grow below ground in pods, similar to a pea or bean. Peanuts are planted in the spring and harvested in the fall and each plant produces about 40 pods with 2 to 3 peanuts in each pod.

64 Cooking with Curious Chef!

65

Utensils
List and pictures of Curious Chef utensils and cookware needed to make the recipe.

Learning by Doing
Additional tips and instructions to facilitate mastering select skills, techniques, and concepts.

Look here for fun and interesting information and activities that connect cooking with what kids learn in school.

Ingredients
List and pictures of ingredients used in the recipe.

Reminder to take pictures of your cooking experience which can be posted at #curiouschef for a chance to be featured on curiouschef.com.

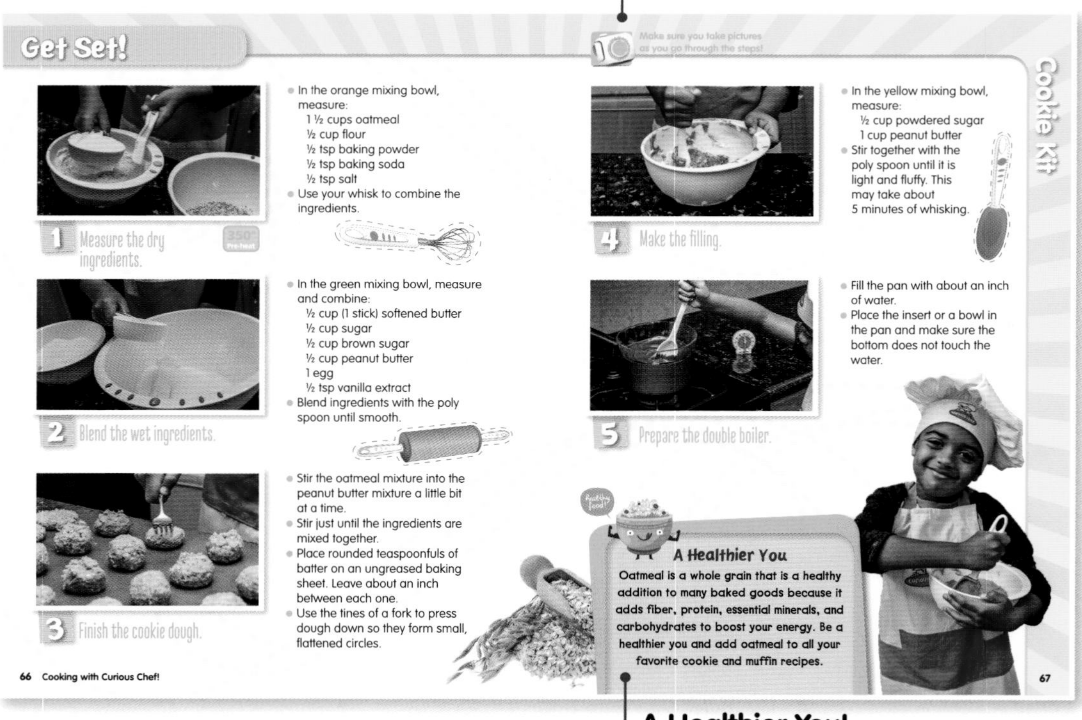

Get Set!

Make sure you take pictures as you go through the steps!

1 Measure the dry ingredients. 350° Pre-heat
- In the orange mixing bowl, measure:
  1 ½ cups oatmeal
  ½ cup flour
  ½ tsp baking powder
  ½ tsp baking soda
  ½ tsp salt
- Use your whisk to combine the ingredients.

2 Blend the wet ingredients.
- In the green mixing bowl, measure and combine:
  ½ cup (1 stick) softened butter
  ½ cup sugar
  ½ cup brown sugar
  ½ cup peanut butter
  1 egg
  ½ tsp vanilla extract
- Blend ingredients with the poly spoon until smooth.

3 Finish the cookie dough.
- Stir the oatmeal mixture into the peanut butter mixture a little bit at a time.
- Stir just until the ingredients are mixed together.
- Place rounded teaspoonfuls of batter on an ungreased baking sheet. Leave about an inch between each one.
- Use the tines of a fork to press dough down so they form small, flattened circles.

4 Make the filling.
- In the yellow mixing bowl, measure:
  ½ cup powdered sugar
  1 cup peanut butter
- Stir together with the poly spoon until it is light and fluffy. This may take about 5 minutes of whisking.

5 Prepare the double boiler.
- Fill the pan with about an inch of water.
- Place the insert or a bowl in the pan and make sure the bottom does not touch the water.

A Healthier You
Oatmeal is a whole grain that is a healthy addition to many baked goods because it adds fiber, protein, essential minerals, and carbohydrates to boost your energy. Be a healthier you and add oatmeal to all your favorite cookie and muffin recipes.

66 Cooking with Curious Chef!

67

A Healthier You!
Additional nutritional tips and suggestions for young chefs so they have the knowledge they need to make healthier food choices.

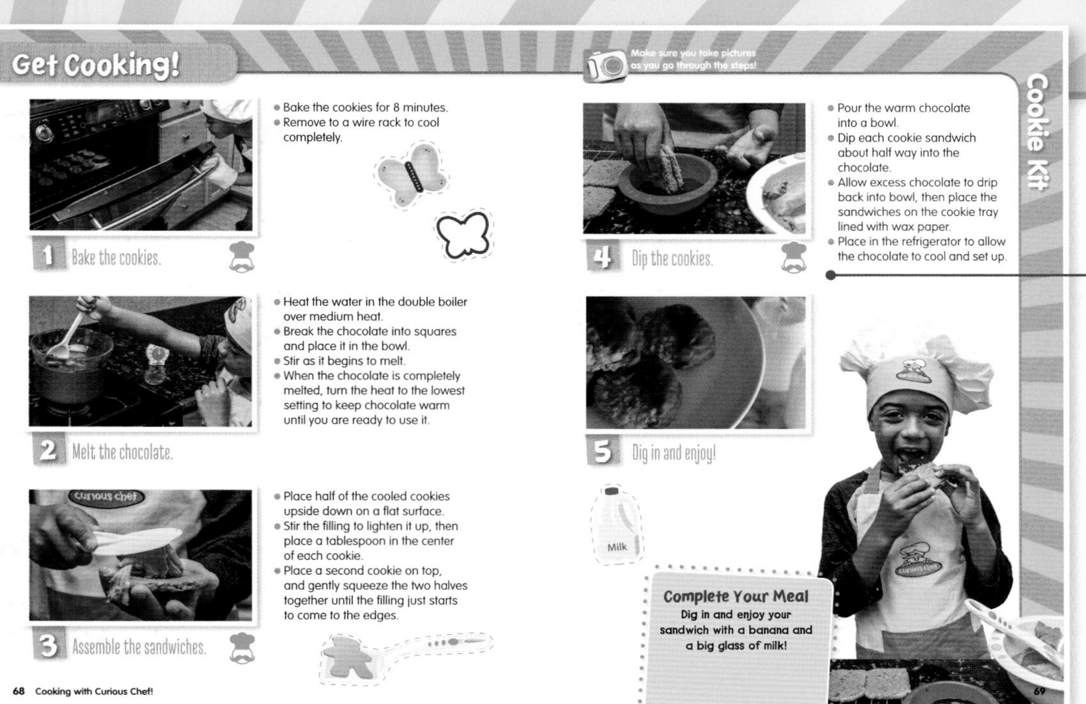
Get Cooking!

Make sure you take pictures as you go through the steps!

1 Bake the cookies.

- Bake the cookies for 8 minutes.
- Remove to a wire rack to cool completely.

2 Melt the chocolate.

- Heat the water in the double boiler over medium heat.
- Break the chocolate into squares and place it in the bowl.
- Stir as it begins to melt.
- When the chocolate is completely melted, turn the heat to the lowest setting to keep chocolate warm until you are ready to use it.

3 Assemble the sandwiches.

- Place half of the cooled cookies upside down on a flat surface.
- Stir the filling to lighten it up, then place a tablespoon in the center of each cookie.
- Place a second cookie on top, and gently squeeze the two halves together until the filling just starts to come to the edges.

4 Dip the cookies.

- Pour the warm chocolate into a bowl.
- Dip each cookie sandwich about half way into the chocolate.
- Allow excess chocolate to drip back into bowl, then place the sandwiches on the cookie tray lined with wax paper.
- Place in the refrigerator to allow the chocolate to cool and set up.

5 Dig in and enjoy!

Complete Your Meal
Dig in and enjoy your sandwich with a banana and a big glass of milk!

Cookie Kit

68 Cooking with Curious Chef!

69

Adult Helper Icon
Steps that should be completed by adults are identified with an adult helper icon.

Each chapter includes a different activity to inspire your young chef's creativity in the kitchen and provides a fun way to use their new skills to explore creative ways to apply their new skills and knowledge.

Get Creative!

Homemade Peanut Butter

Did you know you can make your own peanut butter right at home? It's super easy and fun and takes only a few minutes. You just need peanuts, oil, honey, and a food processor. And if you're really nuts about nuts, get creative with some of the other nuts pictured below and create your own unique nut butter! How does chocolate-macadamia nut butter sound?

What You'll Need:

- 2 ½ cups Spanish peanuts
- 2 tablespoons honey
- 1 tablespoon peanut oil

What You'll Do:

1. Place the peanuts and honey into the bowl of a food processor.
2. Process for 1 minute or until the peanuts are finely chopped.
3. Scrape down the sides of the bowl and continue to process while slowly drizzling in the peanut oil.
4. Process another 1 to 2 minutes or until smooth, stopping now and then to scrap down the sides.

72 Cooking with Curious Chef!

Have Some Fun!

What's My Nickname?

Most of us call the main ingredient in peanut butter, peanuts. But in Georgia, where they grow lots and lots of peanuts, they have a special nickname for this tasty nut. Do you know what it is?

Write the name of each picture in the spaces next to it and the letters inside the box will reveal the answer.

What do Georgians call peanuts?

Cookie Kit

73

Each chapter includes a cooking-related puzzle for kids to complete while they are waiting for things to cook or cool down, or anytime after the cooking is done, just for fun!

Kitchen Safety

At Curious Chef, we understand that a parent's primary concern is their children's safety. That's why we work tirelessly to ensure that our products meet the most stringent safety standards that parents expect and kids deserve. But no matter how safe our products are for young children, there are other safety concerns when working in the kitchen that arise when working with sharp stuff, hot stuff, and germy stuff. Read over the safety tips below with your young chef, answer any questions they may have, and then be confident that your cooking experience will be a safe one.

Sharp Stuff

- Never use a sharp knife without the supervision or permission of an adult.
- When using a cheese grater, be careful to keep your fingers away from the metal bumps.
- Canned food lids are very sharp! Ask an adult helper to remove the lids for you.
- When using a vegetable peeler, be careful to keep your fingers out of the way of the blade.

Hot Stuff

- Always wear oven mitts when placing things in or taking them out of the oven.
- Always turn pan handles toward the middle or back of the stove so you don't accidentally bump the handle and knock over the pan.
- When stirring things in a pan on the stove, always hold on to the pan handle so it doesn't slip off the burner.
- Remember that hot food of any kind can burn you, including water, soups, sauces, butter and oil.

Germy Stuff

- Wash your hands in warm, soapy water before you start cooking.
- Wash your hands in warm, soapy water after handling raw meat, fish, poultry or eggs.
- Wash all utensils, including cutting boards, after using them with raw meat of any kind.
- Do not put cooked meat back on the same plate or tray it was on before you cooked it.
- Wash all fresh fruit and vegetables before using them.

The Adult Helper Icon

Depending on the age of the child, some steps in the preparation of a recipe should be completed by an adult. Steps that require special attention by the adult supervisor are marked with the adult helper icon to indicate it may be a step that children should not complete on their own. However, it is the responsibility of the supervising adult to determine, based on their best judgment, which of the steps the child should be completing on their own, regardless of whether it is marked with this adult helper icon.

Safe-Kitchen Rules

There are just two rules we ask that you follow when preparing the recipes in this book.

Rule #1: Always have a grown-up helper when making the recipes.

Rule #2: Always follow rule #1!

Oatmeal Carrot Muffins

SERVES:
makes 6 muffins

PREP TIME:
20 minutes

READY TO EAT:
50 minutes

Chefs-in-Training

What you'll learn:

- measuring
- grating
- whisking
- mixing
- baking

Shopping List

Got it!

- ○ powdered sugar (2 cups)
- ○ flour (1 cup)
- ○ yogurt (vanilla, ¾ cup)
- ○ oatmeal (½ cup)
- ○ brown sugar (½ cup)
- ○ butter (½ cup softened)
- ○ oil (¼ cup)
- ○ eggs (1)
- ○ carrots (1)
- ○ milk (2 T)
- ○ baking powder (2 tsp)
- ○ vanilla extract (1 tsp)
- ○ cinnamon (¾ tsp)
- ○ baking soda (½ tsp)
- ○ salt (¼ tsp)

Note to Grown Ups

There are few things kids enjoy more than decorating cupcakes, and the Curious Chef decorating set makes it even more fun for young chefs. The frosting tube is oversized, making it easy for little hands to use, and the easy-push plunger helps your child control the frosting flow as they create their special masterpieces!

What's On Your Plate?

Write the ingredients that are part of a healthy plate where they belong on the organizer.

oatmeal

yogurt

oil

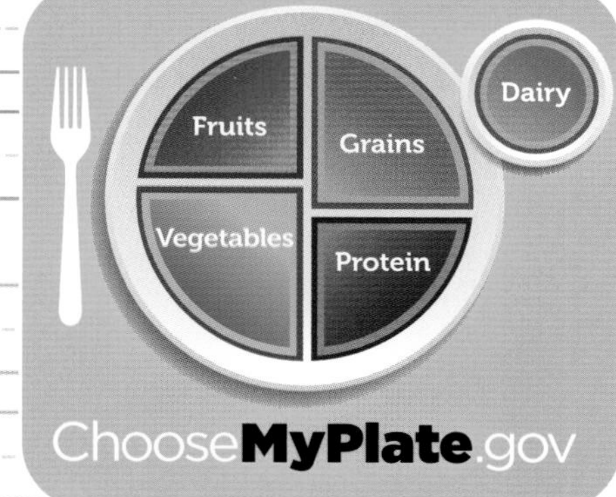

carrots

carrots

Cross out the ingredients that are not part of a healthy plate.

brown sugar

egg

Which ingredient comes from chickens?

Which ingredient comes from cows?

Name the ingredients that come from plants. (hint: There are 4.)

CURIOUS CHEF FOOD FACTS

Sweet and crunchy, eating carrots is like taking a daily vitamin pill. Not only are they an excellent source of vitamins A, B, and C, they are also rich in minerals, fiber, and anti-oxidants. Select young, tender, bright-colored carrots that are firm and crisp. Avoid really big carrots as that may be a sign they are over-mature and won't taste very good.

Get Ready!

Ingredients

flour

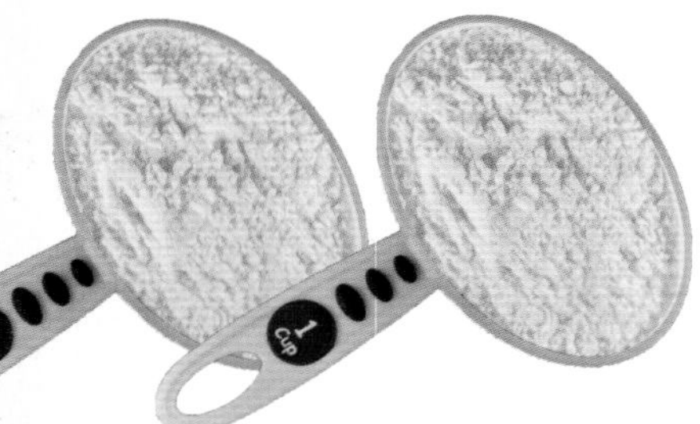

powdered sugar

yogurt

oatmeal

brown sugar

butter

oil

egg

carrots

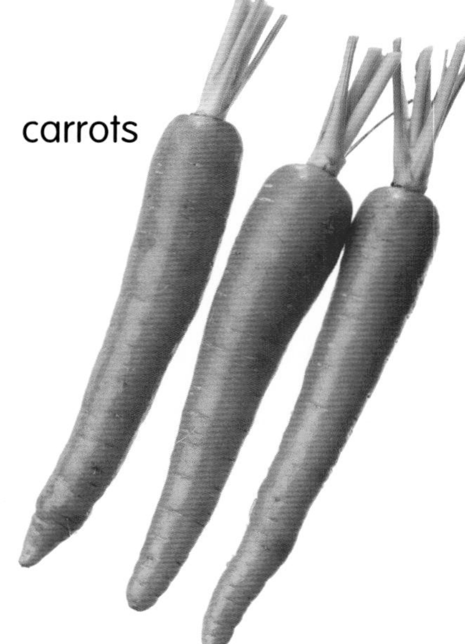

milk

baking powder

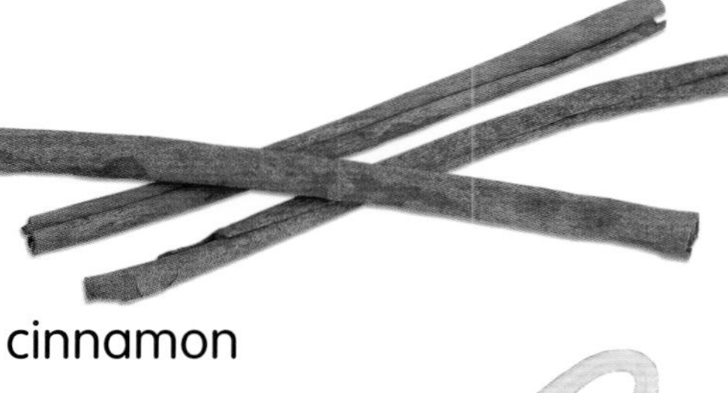

cinnamon

baking soda

vanilla extract

salt

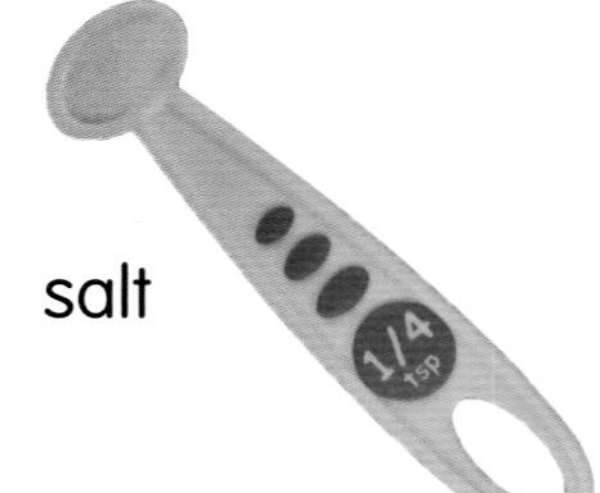

Utensils

Cookware

- muffin tin

- silicone muffin liners

Measurement

- measuring cup set

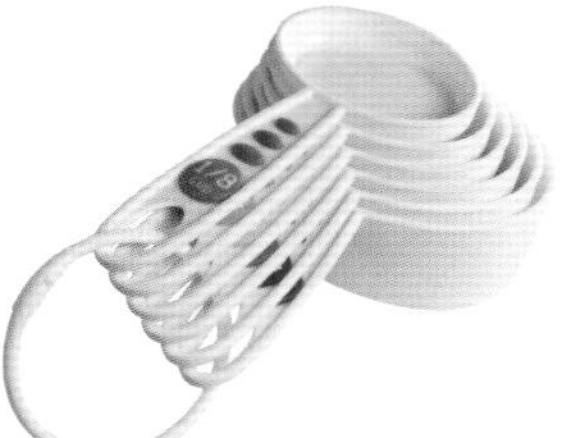

- measuring spoon set

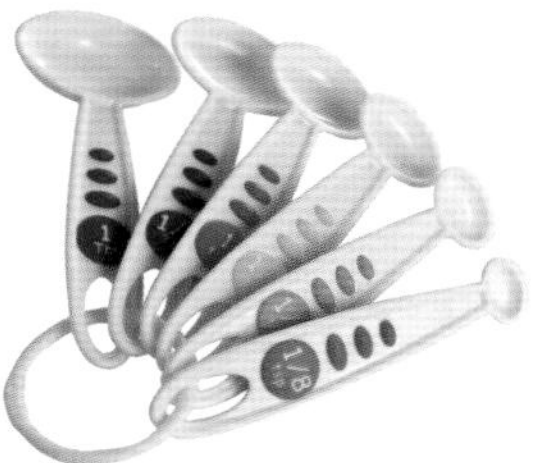

Tools

- whisk

- poly spoon
- silicone mixing spoon

- cheese grater

- prep bowl set

- cutting board

- decorating tube or offset frosting spreader

Other

- 3 qt green mixing bowl
- 2 qt orange mixing bowl

Math Connection

If you double the recipe, how many muffins will it make?

6 muffins + 6 muffins

= ________ muffins

How many eggs will you need?

1 egg + 1 egg

= ________ eggs

Get Set!

Measure the dry ingredients.

- In the orange mixing bowl, measure:
  - 1 cup flour
  - ½ cup brown sugar
  - ½ cup oatmeal
  - 2 tsp baking powder
  - ½ tsp baking soda
  - ¼ teaspoon salt
  - ½ tsp cinnamon

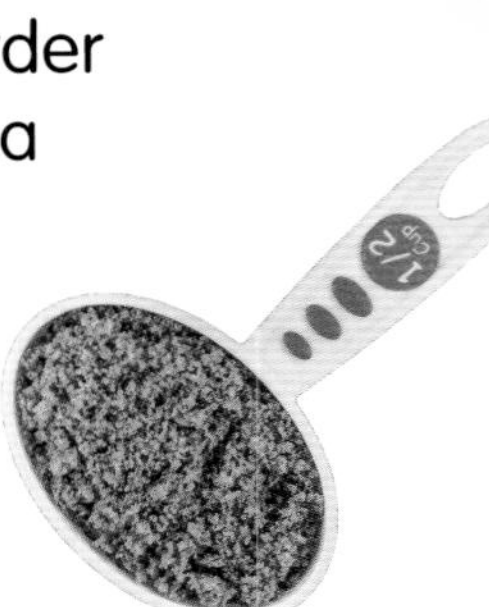

Whisk the eggs.

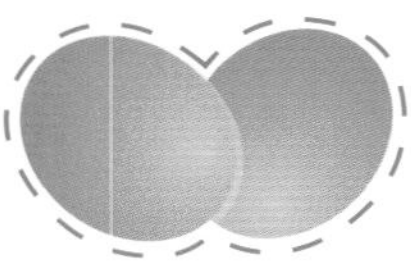

- In the green mixing bowl, crack and whisk the egg.

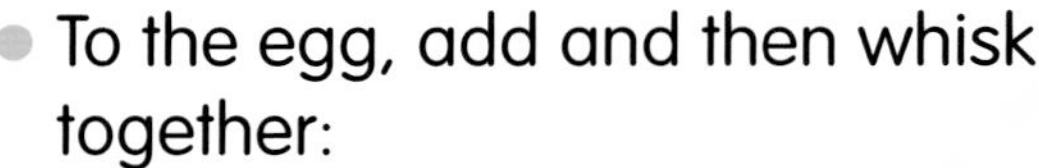

- To the egg, add and then whisk together:
  - ¼ cup vegetable oil
  - ¾ cup yogurt
  - ½ tsp vanilla extract

Measure the wet ingredients.

Make sure you take pictures as you go through the steps!

4 Grate the carrot.

- Grate the carrot and add it to the egg mixture.

5 Finish the batter.

- Add the dry ingredients to the egg mixture. Stir until all the ingredients are combined.

A Healthier You

Vegetables are an important part of a healthy diet, and adding carrots to muffins is a delicious way to get more vegetables into the foods you eat. Be a healthier you and make sure you eat at least 5 servings of fruits and vegetables a day.

Get Cooking!

1 Fill the muffin cups.

- Place one silicone cupcake liner into each of the muffin cups.
- Fill each muffin cup about ⅔ full of batter.

2 Bake the muffins.

- Place the cupcake tin on the middle rack of the preheated oven.
- Set the timer for 25 minutes.

 Make the frosting.

- Into the green mixing bowl, measure:
  - ½ cup softened butter
  - 2 cups powdered sugar
  - ½ teaspoon vanilla
  - ¼ teaspoon cinnamon
  - 2 tablespoons milk
- Stir the mixture with the poly spoon until the butter is smooth and ingredients are thoroughly combined.
- Add another tablespoon or two of milk to reach desired consistency.

Make sure you take pictures as you go through the steps!

4 Test for doneness.

- When the timer goes off, test the muffins to make sure they are done.
  - Insert a toothpick or butter knife into the center of a muffin.
  - If it comes out clean the muffins are done.
  - If it comes out with gooey batter on it, allow them to cook for a few more minutes.

5 Cool and frost.

- Allow the muffins to cool in the cupcake tin for 2–3 minutes.
- Remove them to a wire rack to cool completely.
- Use your decorating tube or offset frosting spreader to decorate the cooled muffins.

6 Dig in and enjoy!

Complete Your Meal

Dig in and enjoy with fresh fruit and yogurt!

Practice Makes Perfect!

Vanilla Cupcakes

SERVES: makes 6 cupcakes

PREP TIME: 20 minutes

READY TO EAT: 1 hour

Get Ready!

Ingredients

- 2 cups powdered sugar
- ¾ cups flour
- 6 T butter, melted
- 4 oz cream cheese
- 1 egg
- ⅓ cup granulated sugar
- ¼ cup butter, softened
- ¼ cup milk
- 2 tsp cream (half-n-half)
- 2 tsp vanilla extract
- 1 tsp baking powder
- ⅛ tsp salt
- food coloring

Utensils

- mixing bowl set
- measuring cup set
- measuring spoon set
- whisk
- silicone mixing spatula
- poly spoon
- cupcake tin
- silicone cupcake liners
- decorator set
- wire cooling rack

Get Set!

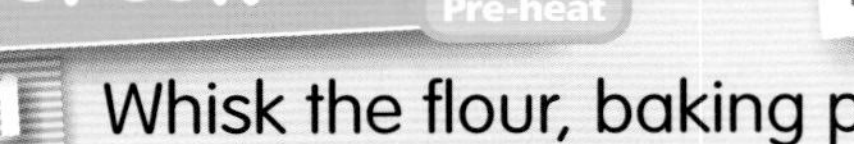

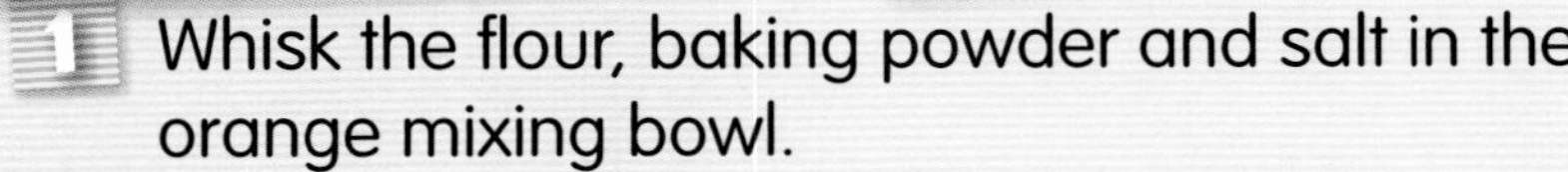

1. Whisk the flour, baking powder and salt in the orange mixing bowl.
2. In the green mixing bowl, whisk the egg and granulated sugar until light and foamy. Then whisk in the melted butter, milk and 1 tsp vanilla extract.
3. Gradually fold in the flour mixture.
4. Place the cupcake liners in the cupcake tin.
5. Fill the cupcake liners about ¾-full of batter.

Get Cooking!

1. Bake cupcakes for 18–20 minutes or until they turn light golden brown. Test for doneness by inserting a toothpick in the middle of a cupcake. Cool on a wire rack.
2. Combine the cream cheese, softened butter, cream, and 1 teaspoon vanilla in the orange mixing bowl and beat with your poly spoon until smooth and fluffy. Gradually beat in the powdered sugar until smooth and spreadable. Add a few drops of food coloring and stir until it is evenly distributed.
3. When the cupcakes are completely cooled, frost using the decorating set.

Egg and Cheese Breakfast Bites

SERVES: makes 12 muffins

PREP TIME: 20 minutes 

READY TO EAT: 45 minutes

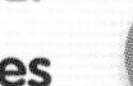

Get Ready!

Ingredients

- 6 eggs
- 4 oz cheddar cheese
- ½ cup cooked ham, bacon or sausage
- ¼ cup fresh spinach
- ¼ cup bell pepper
- 2 T fresh chives
- 1 T onion
- ¼ tsp salt
- dash pepper

Utensils

- muffin tin
- silicone cupcake liners
- measuring cup set
- measuring spoon set
- nylon plastic knife
- poly spoon
- cheese grater
- whisk
- 2 qt orange mixing bowl

Get Set!

1. Whisk the eggs in the orange mixing bowl.
2. Measure the salt into eggs.
3. Finely dice the vegetables (and the ham if using). Add to the eggs.
4. Grate the cheese. Add to the eggs.
5. Use the poly spoon to combine all the ingredients.
6. Line each muffin cup with a silicone cupcake liner.
7. Scoop ⅓ cup of the mixture into each muffin cup.

Get Cooking!

1. Place the muffins on the middle rack of the preheated oven.
2. Bake for 20–30 minutes.
3. Test for doneness.
4. Allow muffins to cool for 5 minutes.
5. Dig in and enjoy with whole-grain toast and 100% fruit juice!

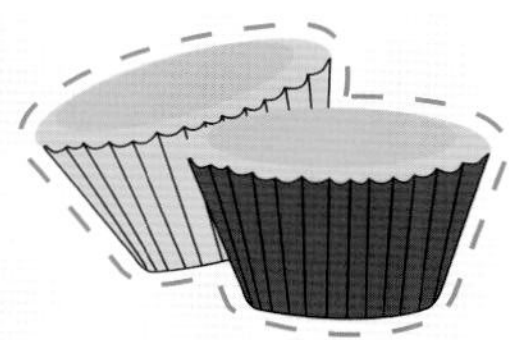

Get Creative!

You're the Chef!

Oatmeal muffins can be made with all kinds of ingredients. Check out the ingredients below. Pretend you own a restaurant. Choose ingredients to create new muffins for your menu. Name each muffin and write a description below.

apples

zucchini

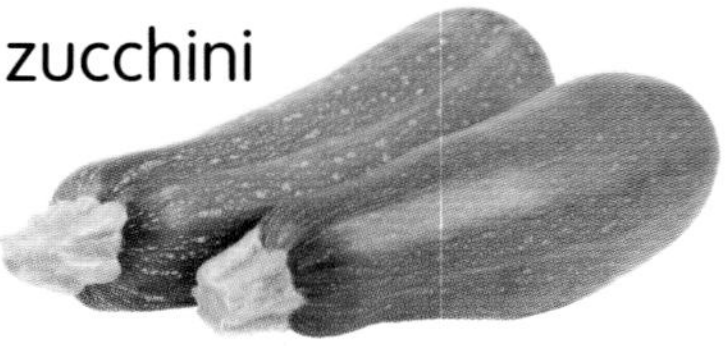

currants

raisins

bananas

granola

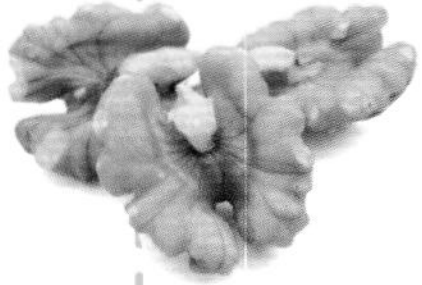

walnuts

cranberries

chocolate chips

raspberries

blueberries

sunflower seeds

strawberries

beets

My Creation

My Creation

Have Some Fun!

Rhyme Time

Find cooking words that rhyme with each word below.

Find rhyming words in the Get Ready! section on pages 16–17.

power _____ _____ _____ _____ _____

flutter _____ _____ _____ _____ _____ _____

fault _____ _____ _____ _____

pin _____ _____ _____

loon _____ _____ _____ _____ _____

tease _____ _____ _____ _____ _____ _____

Find rhyming words in the Get Set! section on pages 18–19.

treasure _____ _____ _____ _____ _____ _____ _____

risk _____ _____ _____ _____ _____

trait _____ _____ _____ _____ _____

cry _____ _____ _____

legs _____ _____ _____ _____

matter _____ _____ _____ _____ _____ _____

Find rhyming words in the Get Cooking! section on pages 20–21.

will _____ _____ _____ _____

cake _____ _____ _____ _____

rest _____ _____ _____ _____

pool _____ _____ _____ _____

hole _____ _____ _____ _____

lost _____ _____ _____ _____ _____

Challenge:

Write sentences using the pairs of rhyming words. And don't worry about making sense! Just have some fun and see how creative you can get.

Example: foil/oil;
I wrapped the oil in foil.

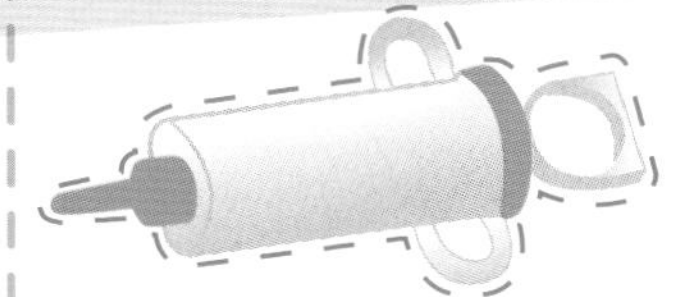

Fruit Pizza

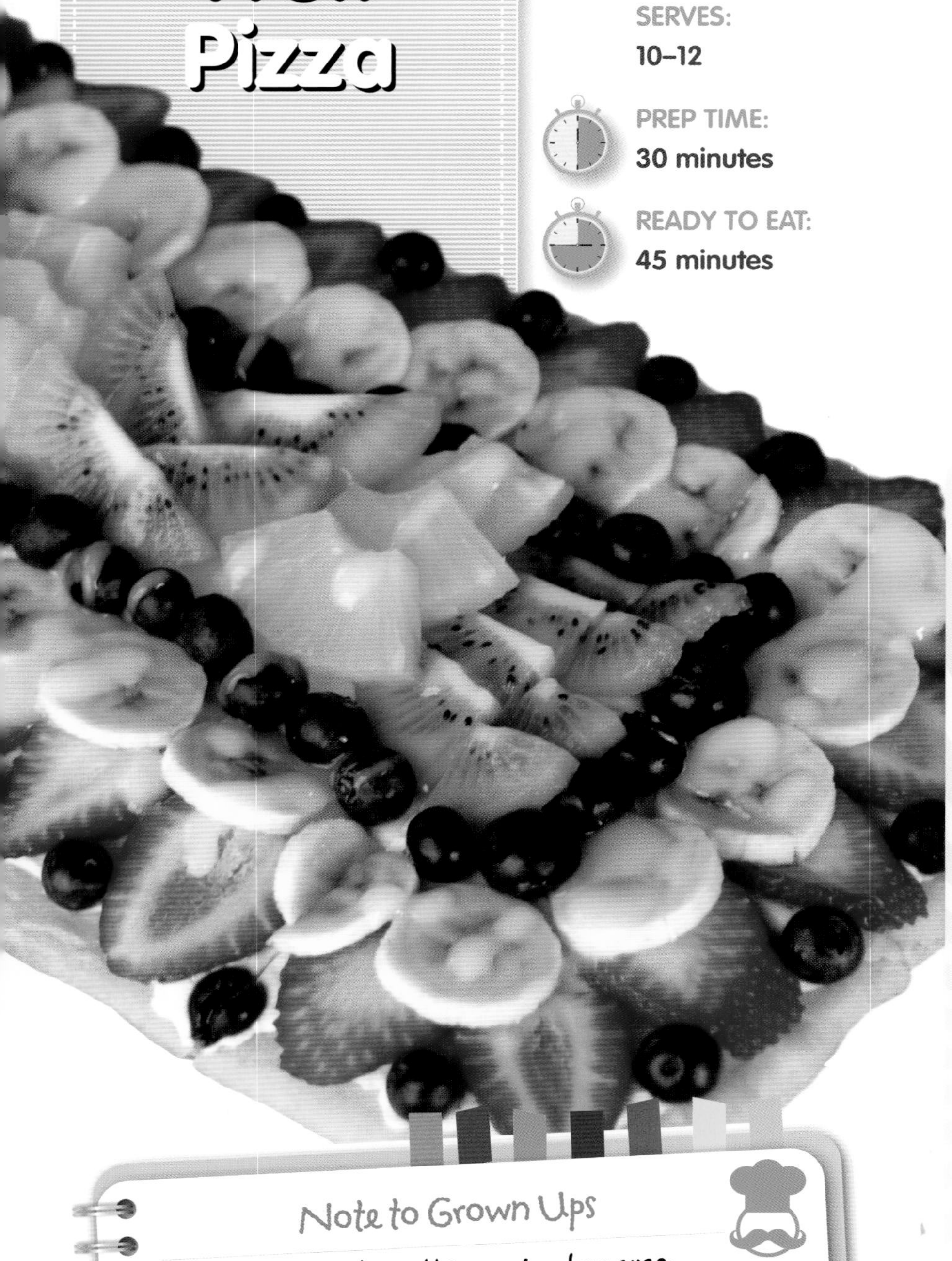

SERVES:
10–12

PREP TIME:
30 minutes

READY TO EAT:
45 minutes

Chefs-in-Training

What you'll learn:

- slicing
- stirring
- spreading frosting
- measuring
- food safety

Shopping List

Got it!

- ○ canned pineapple (15-oz can)
- ○ refrigerated crescent roll dough (1 can)
- ○ cream cheese (8 ounces)
- ○ powdered sugar (½ cup)
- ○ blueberries (½ cup)
- ○ strawberries (8–10)
- ○ banana (1)
- ○ kiwi (1)
- ○ cornstarch (2 T)

Note to Grown Ups

Kids love making this recipe because they can do so many of the steps all on their own. You may need to help with peeling the kiwi, but your sous chef should be able to prep all the other fruit themselves using the nylon plastic knife. Use the offset frosting spreader and even the youngest chefs-in-training can enjoy success with that step as well.

crescent rolls

What's On Your Plate?

Write the ingredients that are part of a healthy plate where they belong on the organizer.

pineapple

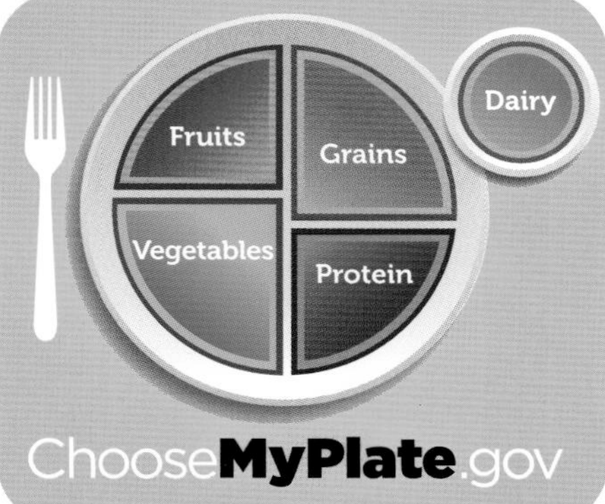

banana

Cross out the ingredients that are not part of a healthy plate.

cream cheese

kiwi

blueberries

powdered sugar

strawberries

Which ingredient is a solid fat?

Which ingredient is made from refined flour?

CURIOUS CHEF FOOD FACTS

When you eat food that is high in calories but low in nutritional value, you are eating "empty calories." Solid fats like butter and cream cheese contain a lot of empty calories. Eating a small amount of empty calories is ok, but try to eat as little as possible.

Get Ready!

Ingredients

crescent roll dough

cream cheese

powdered sugar

cornstarch

canned pineapple

kiwi

blueberries

strawberries

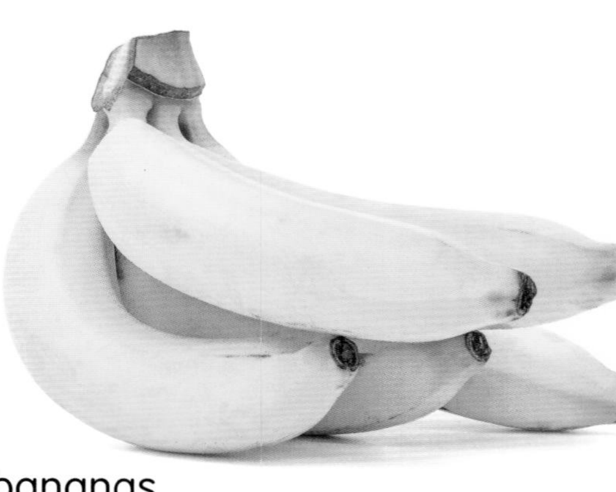
bananas

Utensils

Cookware

- cookie sheet

- sauce pan (small)

Measurement

- measuring cup set

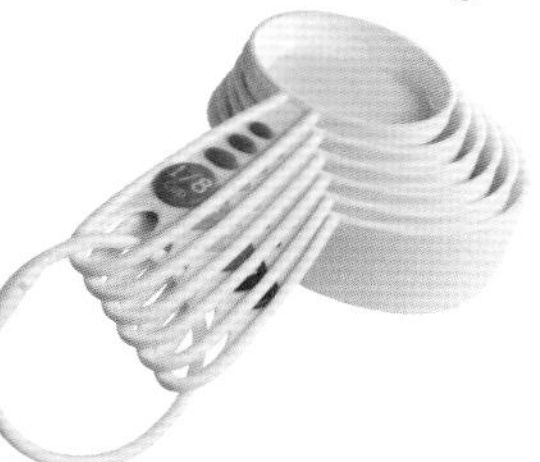

- measuring spoon set

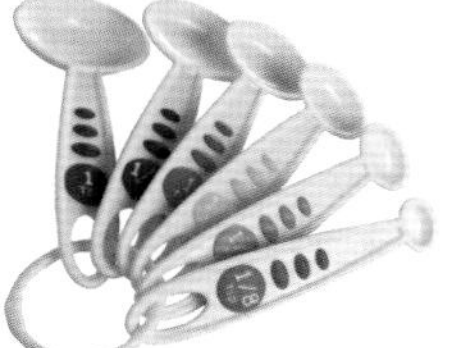

- clear measuring cup

Tools

- pizza cutter
- poly spoon

- nylon plastic knife

- whisk

- offset frosting spreader

Other

- 2 qt orange mixing bowl
- 1 qt yellow mixing bowl
- prep bowl set
- colander

- cutting board

Cultural Connection

Pizza is thought to have originated in Naples, Italy. In 1889, a restaurant owner baked what he called "pizza" especially for the visit of Italian King Umberto I and Queen Margherita. He topped the pizza with mozzarella cheese, basil and tomatoes to represent the three colors of the Italian flag. The queen liked it so much that they named the pizza after her. Today, Margherita pizza is one of the most popular pizzas ordered in restaurants.

Get Set!

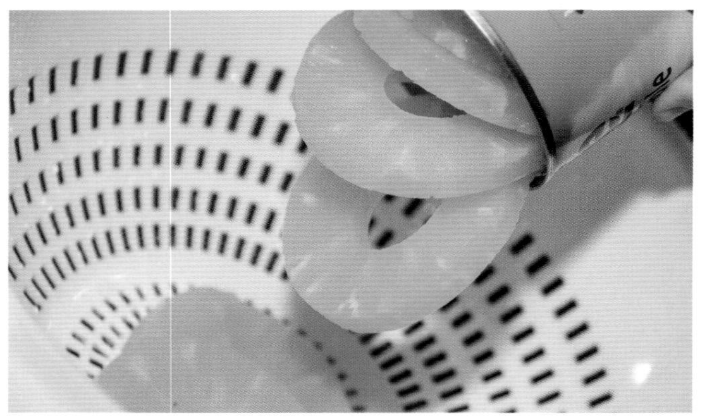

1 Drain the pineapple.

- Drain the pineapple over the mixing bowl. Save the juice for later.

Learning by Doing

To drain canned items, place a colander over a bowl and slowly pour the contents into the colander.

2 Make the frosting.

- In the mixing bowl, use the poly spoon to combine:
  softened cream cheese
  ½ cup powdered sugar
  2 tablespoons pineapple juice

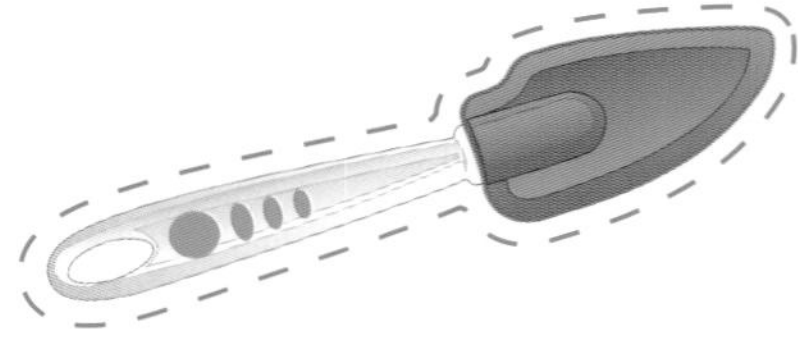

3 Wash the fruit.

- Rinse the strawberries and blueberries in a colander under cold running water.
- Shake to remove excess water, then pat dry with a paper towel.

Make sure you take pictures as you go through the steps!

4 Peel and slice fruit.

- Peel the kiwi.
- Slice the kiwi into thin slices.
- Peel and slice the banana into thin slices.
- Remove the stems from the strawberries and slice into thin slices.

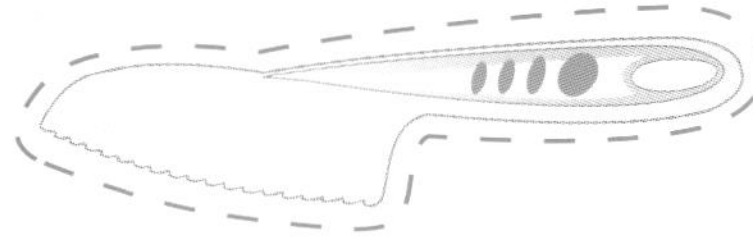

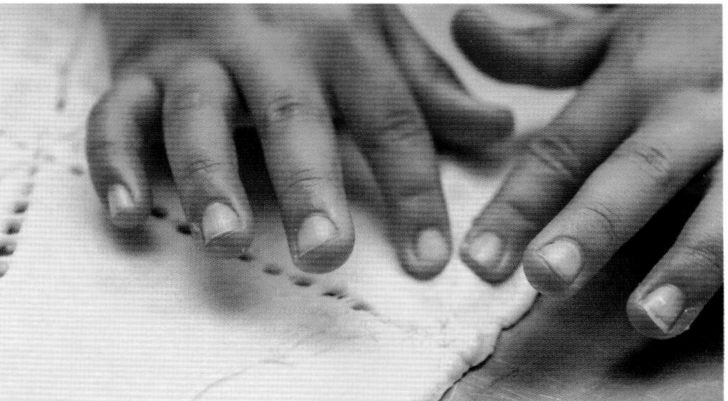

5 Prepare the crust.

- Unroll the crescent roll dough onto an ungreased cookie sheet.
- Press the seams together to form a solid crust with no holes in the seams.

A Healthier You

Fruit comes in lots of colors, and different colored fruits have different kinds of nutrients. Be a healthier you and eat a variety of colors of fruit to make sure you get a healthy mix of all the nutrients these yummy treats have to offer.

Get Cooking!

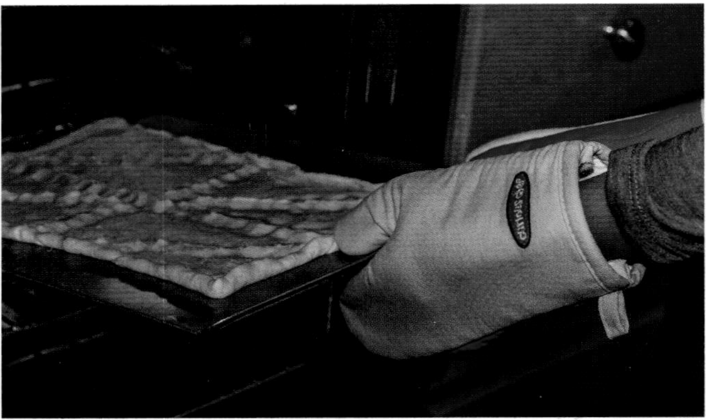

1 Bake the crust.

- Bake the dough according to the package directions.

2 Make the glaze.

- To the sauce pan, add:
  the remaining pineapple juice
  2 tablespoons cornstarch
- Cook over medium heat, stirring often with a whisk, until the mixture thickens.
- Pour glaze into the clear measuring cup.

Learning by Doing

Add more hot water, 1 teaspoon at a time, if the glaze is too thick.

3 Spread the frosting.

- When the crust has cooled, spread the frosting evenly over the crust using the offset frosting spreader.

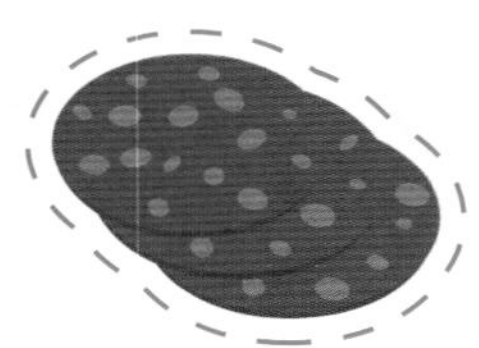

Make sure you take pictures as you go through the steps!

4 Add fruit toppings.

- Arrange the fruit in a fun pattern on the frosting.

5 Drizzle with the glaze.

- Drizzle the glaze over the fruit to make a pretty design.

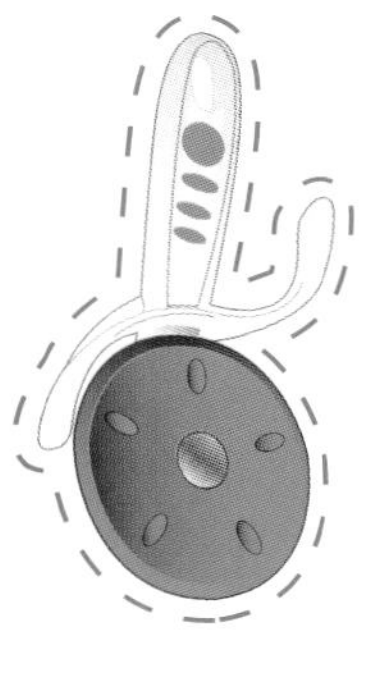

6 Dig in and enjoy!

- Cut pizza into serving-sized squares with your pizza cutter.

Complete Your Meal

Dig in and enjoy with yogurt or a big glass of milk!

Practice Makes Perfect!

Breakfast Pizza

SERVES:
6–8

PREP TIME:
20 minutes

READY TO EAT:
45 minutes

Get Ready!

Ingredients

- 6 eggs (whisked)
- 1 pkg crescent roll dough
- ¾ lb breakfast sausage, cooked
- 1 packet country gravy mix
- 1 T butter
- 8 oz grated cheddar cheese
- 4 oz grated Monterey Jack cheese
- orange juice (optional)

Utensils

- baking sheet
- large skillet
- cheese grater
- sauce pan (small)
- cookie turner
- nylon plastic knife
- whisk
- 2 qt orange mixing bowl
- pastry brush
- cutting board

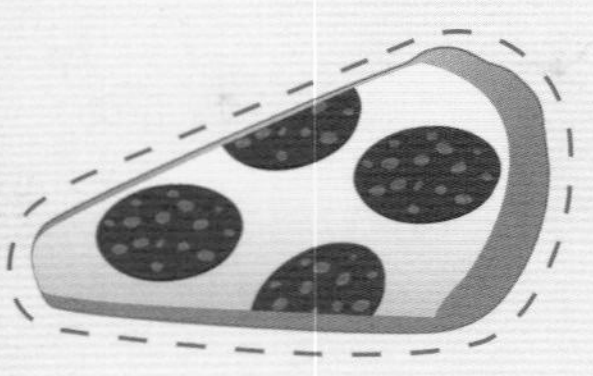

Get Set!

1. Roll crescent roll dough out onto a greased baking sheet. Press the seams together to seal.

Get Cooking!

1. Bake the crust for 11–13 minutes or until it just begins to brown.
2. Prepare gravy according to the directions on the package.
3. Melt butter in the large skillet. Add the whisked eggs, season with salt and pepper and cook and stir the eggs until they just begin to firm up.
4. Use a pastry brush to spread the gravy over the crust. Top with the eggs, sausage, and cheese.
5. Bake 5–10 minutes longer or until the eggs are set and the cheese is melted.
6. Dig in and enjoy with fresh squeezed orange juice!

Taco Pizza

SERVES: 6

PREP TIME: 20 minutes

READY TO EAT: 35 minutes

Get Ready!

Ingredients

- 1 lb ground beef
- 1 can refrigerated pizza dough
- 1 can refried beans
- 1 cup tomato salsa
- 8 oz cheddar cheese, grated
- 2 tomatoes, diced
- 1 pkg taco seasoning
- ½ head iceberg lettuce
- 4-oz can sliced olives
- taco sauce
- carrots (optional)
- celery sticks (optional)

Utensils

- large skillet
- pizza pan
- silicone mixing spoon
- measuring cup set
- cookie turner
- nylon plastic knife
- 2 qt orange mixing bowl
- cheese grater
- offset frosting spreader
- cutting board

Get Set!

400° Pre-heat

1. Finely chop the lettuce.
2. In the orange mixing bowl, combine the beans and salsa.
3. Unroll the pizza dough onto an ungreased pizza pan.

Get Cooking!

1. Bake the crust for 5 minutes.
2. Brown the ground beef in a large skillet. Add the taco seasoning mix according to package directions.
3. Heat the beans and salsa in the microwave to soften. Use the offset frosting spreader to spread the bean mixture evenly over the partially baked crust.
4. Top with beef, olives, and cheese.
5. Bake for another 10–15 minutes.
6. Allow pizza to cool slightly, then top with lettuce, tomatoes and taco sauce.
7. Dig in and enjoy with carrot and celery sticks!

Get Creative!

Fun with Fruit

There are lots of ways to enjoy cut up fruit. Check out the recipes below. Can you think of other creative ways to use cut up fruit? Use your culinary imagination and invent your own recipes using your favorite fruit.

Fresh Fruit Infused Water

Making fruit infused water is as easy as combining fresh sliced fruit, herbs, water, and ice. Make it in a large pitcher and you will always have ice-cold flavored water on hand in the fridge for a healthy alternative to soda or sweetened juice.

Here are some suggested combinations to experiment with:

- lemon, orange, lime
- raspberry, lemon, or lime
- pineapple and fresh mint
- blackberry and fresh sage leaves
- watermelon and fresh rosemary
- cucumber and lemon

Fresh Fruit Smoothies

Smoothies can be made by combining yogurt, milk or juice, ice, and fruit of your choice in a blender. The basic recipe is: ½ cup vanilla or fruit-flavored yogurt, ½ to 1 cup milk or juice, ½ cup crushed ice or 1 cup ice cubes, 1–2 cups cut up fruit of your choice.

Fresh Fruit Salad

Toss cut up fruit with sour cream, cool whip, and mini marshmallows.

Fresh Fruit Boats

Cut a watermelon or other large melon in half and scoop out the fruit to form a bowl. Cut up a collection of your favorite fruit and serve it up in the hollowed-out melon.

Fresh Fruit Kebabs

Place a collection of your favorite cut up fruit on wooden skewers.

IMPORTANT SAFETY INFORMATION:
Wash the peel of all fruit well to remove any harmful bacteria.

Odd Ingredient Out

Eating foods from each of the 5 food groups is important for a healthy diet. Look at the groups of food below. Each group includes one food that does not belong. Cross out the wrong food and then add it to the group it belongs in.

Fruit Group

apple grapes chicken banana

Veggie Group

rice broccoli zucchini potato

Grains Group

bread crackers pasta ice cream

Protein Group

nuts cheese eggs lettuce

Dairy Group

milk yogurt strawberry cheese

Banana Cream Pie

SERVES:
8

PREP TIME:
30 minutes

READY TO EAT:
1 hour 30 minutes

Chefs-in-Training

What you'll learn:
- making pie crust
- separating eggs
- making custard
- measuring skills
- whipping cream

Shopping List

Got it!

- ○ whole milk (3 cups)
- ○ eggs (3)
- ○ bananas (2)
- ○ flour (1 ½ cups)
- ○ whipping cream (1 cup)
- ○ sugar (1 cup + 2 T)
- ○ shortening (1/3 cup)
- ○ cornstarch (¼ cup)
- ○ baking chocolate (4 oz; optional)
- ○ butter (3 T)
- ○ salt (1 ½ tsp)
- ○ vanilla extract (2 tsp)

Note to Grown Ups

While many people are intimidated by the thought of making homemade pie crust, using Curious Chef tools makes it possible for kids to do it with ease. The nonstick rolling pin is weighted to make rolling out dough not only fun, but easy too! And your young chef will be so proud when they can dish up each piece themselves using their very own pie server designed with an ergonomic handle for small hands.

What's On Your Plate?

Write the ingredients that are part of a healthy plate where they belong on the organizer.

bananas

eggs

flour

butter

milk

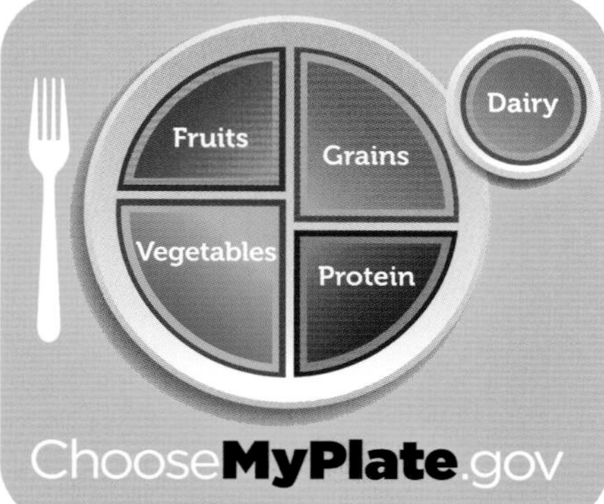

bananas

Cross out the ingredients that are not part of a healthy plate.

milk

whipping cream

sugar

Name the two ingredients that are made from milk.

Which ingredient is a healthy source of calcium?

A Healthier You

Reduced-fat milk contains the same amount of calcium as whole milk, but with less fat calories. A healthy diet includes three 8-ounce servings of dairy products a day, so be a healthier you and choose reduced or fat-free dairy products.

Get Ready!

Ingredients

bananas

eggs

milk

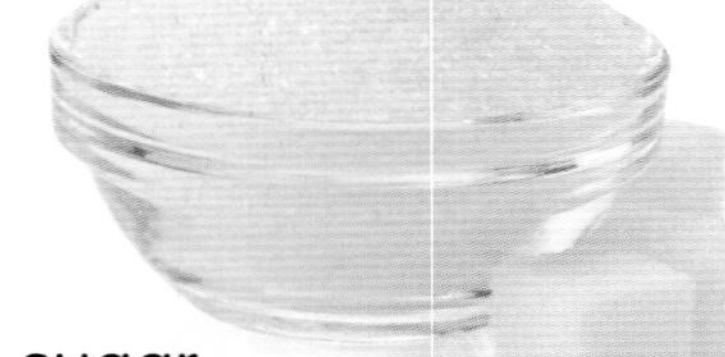

sugar

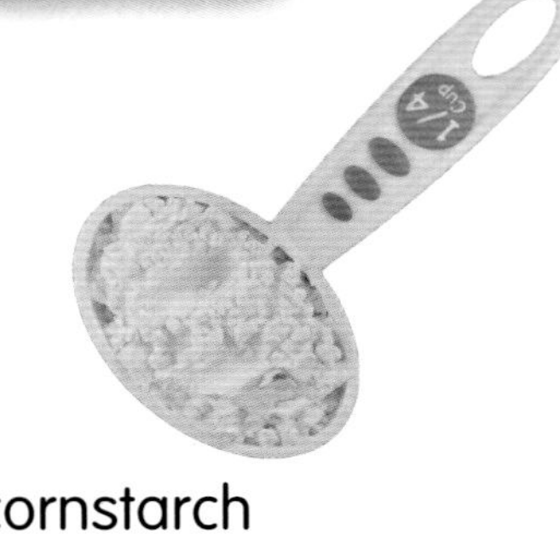

cornstarch

butter

vanilla extract

flour

shortening

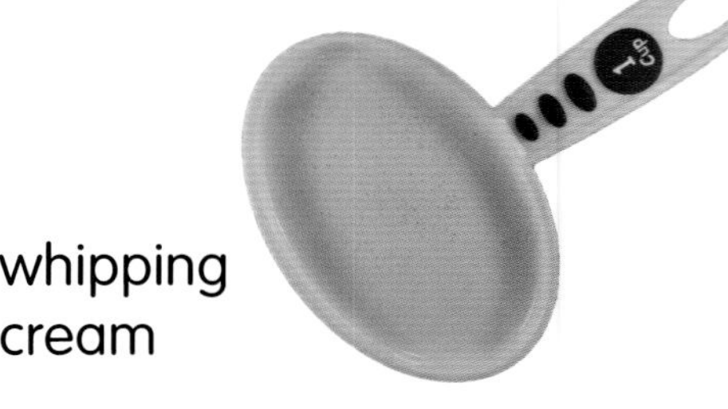

whipping cream

salt

baking chocolate (optional)

Utensils

Cookware

- metal pie tin

- saucepan (large)

Measurement

- measuring cup set

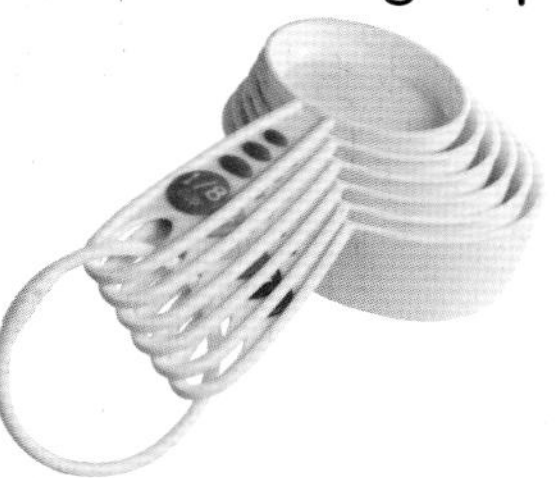

- measuring spoon set

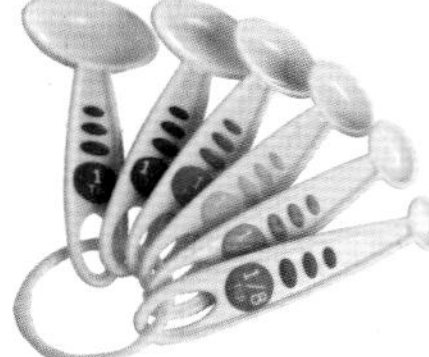

- clear measuring cup

Tools

- poly spoon

- whisk

- nylon plastic knife

- rolling pin

- nylon pie server

- cheese grater (optional)

Other

- mixing bowl set
- handheld mixer
- prep bowl set
- pinch bowl set

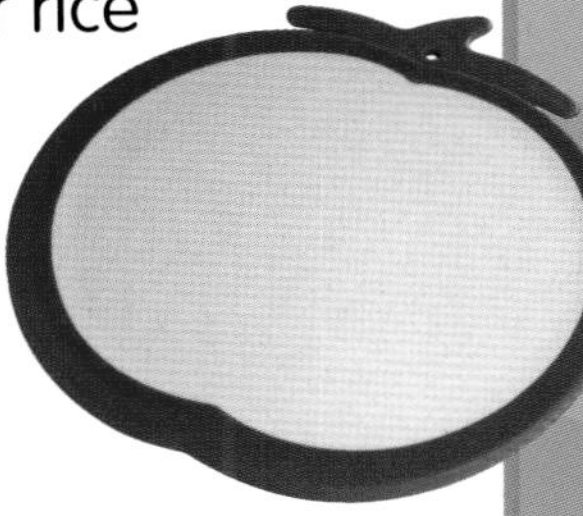

- parchment or wax paper
- pie weights, dried beans, or rice
- cutting board
- plastic wrap

Science Connection

When you whip cream from a liquid into a solid "whipped cream", you are watching science in action. When you whip the cream, you are actually rearranging the fat molecules in such a way that they trap air bubbles that are created by the whipping action in a protective "shell" that keeps the bubbles from popping. It's all those trapped air bubbles that turn the liquid cream into fluffy "whipped" cream.

Get Set!

 Make the pie crust. 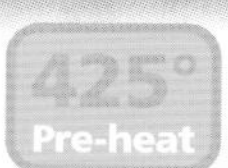

425° Pre-heat

- In the green mixing bowl, measure 1 ½ cups flour, ⅓ cup shortening and 1 tsp salt.
- Mix together with a fork until it looks like coarse sand.
- Add 5–6 tablespoons of water, 1–2 at a time, until the dough sticks together in a ball.
- Form into a disc, wrap in plastic, and chill for 15 minutes.

2 Prepare the custard filling.

- In the large saucepan, measure and whisk together:
  1 cup sugar
  ¼ cup cornstarch
  ½ teaspoon salt

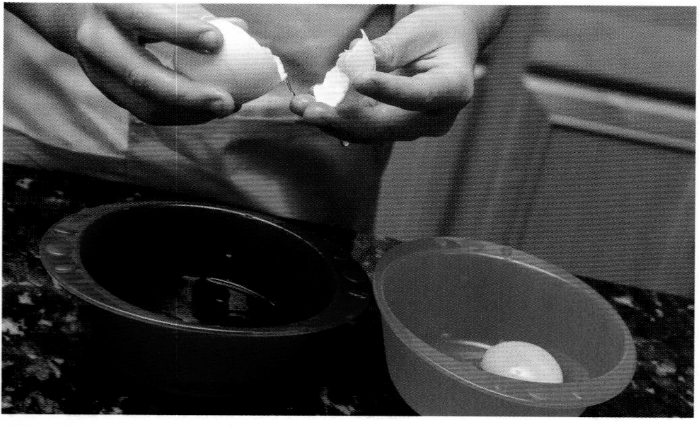

3 Separate the egg yolks.

- Separate the eggs.
- Place the yolks in the prep bowl.

Learning by Doing

Crack the egg, then transfer the yolk back and forth between the shell halves allowing the white to drip into one bowl.

Make sure you take pictures as you go through the steps!

4 Prepare the bananas.

- Slice the bananas into thin slices.
- Arrange bananas in a single layer on a plate and cover with plastic wrap to keep them from turning brown.

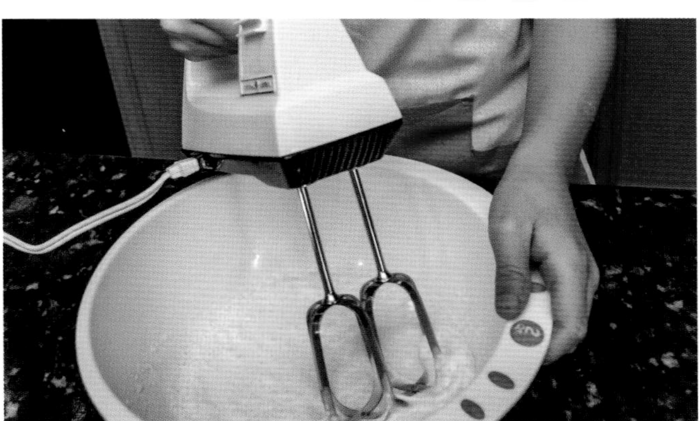

5 Make the whipped cream topping.

- In the orange mixing bowl, combine:
  - 1 cup whipping cream
  - 2 tablespoons sugar
  - 1 teaspoon vanilla extract
- Using an electric mixer, whip the cream until soft peaks form.
- Chill in the refrigerator.

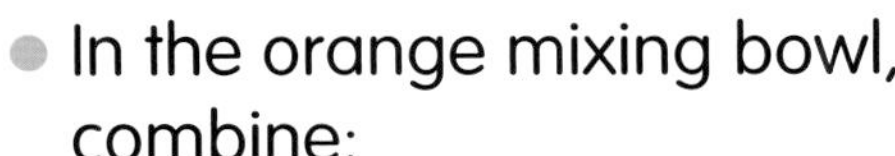

6 Roll out the dough.

- On a floured surface, roll the dough into a 13-inch circle and place in the pie tin.
- Pinch around the edges to form a thick outer rim.

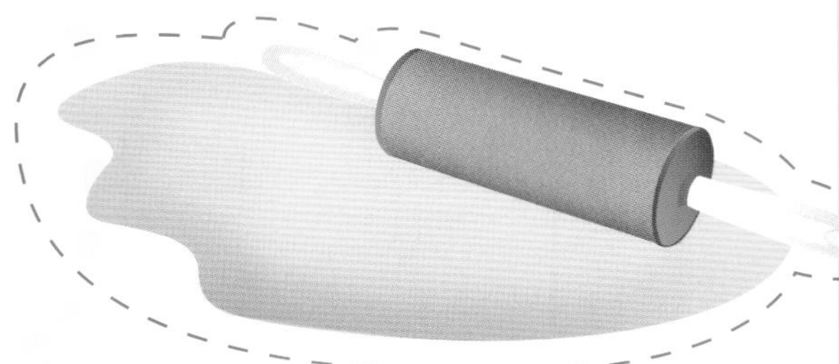

Get Cooking!

1 Bake the crust.

- Cover the crust with parchment or wax paper.
- Cover the paper with a layer of pie weights, dried beans, or rice.
- Bake at 425°F for 12 minutes.
- Remove the paper and weights.
- Reduce heat to 350°F and bake another 10–15 minutes or until the crust is lightly browned.

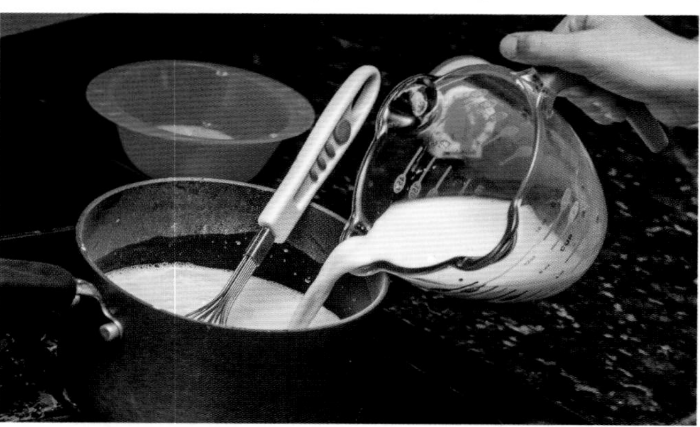

2 Cook the custard filling.

- Stir 3 cups milk into the sugar and cornstarch mixture.
- Cook over medium heat until thickened.
- Reduce heat and cook another 2 minutes.
- Stir a small amount of custard into the egg yolks, then return to the pan.
- Cook another 2 minutes.

MILK

3 Finish making the custard.

- Remove the custard from the stove.
- Stir in 3 tablespoons butter and 1 teaspoon vanilla extract.
- Allow to cool.

Make sure you take pictures as you go through the steps!

4 Assemble the pie.

- Pour half of the custard into the cooked pie crust.
- Arrange sliced bananas over the custard.
- Pour the remaining custard over the bananas.
- Allow to cool in the refrigerator.

5 Finish the pie.

- When the custard has completely cooled, spread the whipped cream over the pie.
- Grate baking chocolate over the top. (optional)

6 Dig in and enjoy!

- Cut into eight pieces and serve it up with the nylon pie server.

Complete Your Meal

Dig in and enjoy with fresh fruit and a big glass of milk!

Practice Makes Perfect!

Chicken Pot Pie

SERVES: 6–8

PREP TIME: 20 minutes 

READY TO EAT: 1 hour 

Get Ready!

Ingredients

- 2 ⅔ cups flour
- ⅔ cup shortening
- 2 cups cubed cooked chicken
- 14.5-oz can cream of chicken soup
- 12-oz package mixed vegetables (carrots, peas, green beans, corn)
- ½ cup milk
- 1 tsp dried thyme
- 1 tsp poultry seasoning
- 2 tsp salt
- ¼ tsp pepper

Utensils

- metal pie tin
- rolling pin
- silicone mixing spoon
- mixing bowl set
- pastry wheel
- measuring cup set
- measuring spoon set

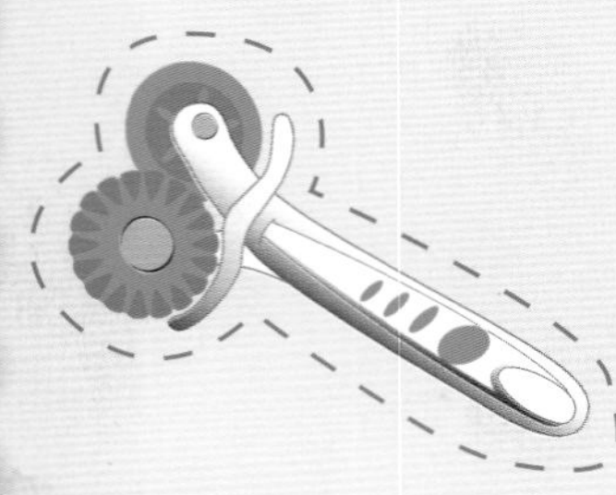

Get Set!

1. In the orange mixing bowl combine the flour, shortening and 1 teaspoon salt.
2. Mix together with a fork until it looks like coarse sand.
3. Add 10–12 tablespoons of water, 1–2 at a time, until the dough sticks together in a ball.
4. Form into two discs and wrap in plastic wrap.
5. Chill in the refrigerator for 15 minutes.
6. Roll out one of the discs and place in the greased pie tin.
7. Roll out the other disc into a 10-inch circle, then cut it into ½-inch strips using the pastry wheel.
8. Add the remaining ingredients to the green mixing bowl. Stir to thoroughly combine. Pour into the pie tin.
9. Arrange the strips of crust over the filling in an open-weave, crisscross pattern.

Get Cooking!

1. Bake the pie for 35–45 minutes or until the crust is lightly browned and the filling is bubbling.
2. Allow pie to cool for 10 minutes before serving.
3. Dig in and enjoy with a fresh green salad!

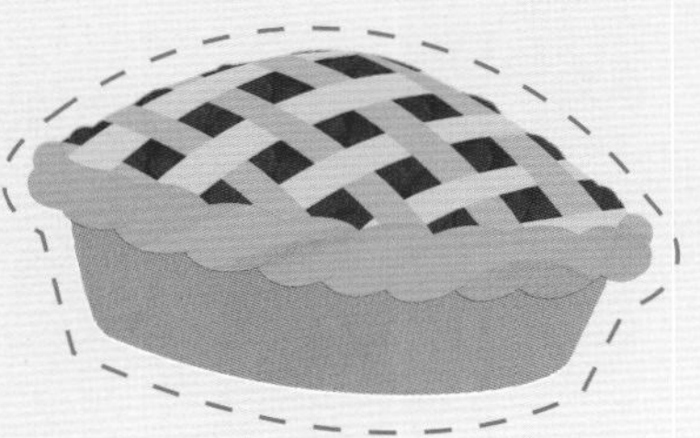

Cherry Pie

SERVES: 8

PREP TIME: 20 minutes 

READY TO EAT: 1 hour 20 minutes

Get Ready!

Ingredients

- 2 ½ cups flour
- 2 21-oz cans cherry pie filling
- ⅔ cup shortening
- 1 tsp sugar
- ½ tsp cinnamon
- vanilla ice cream (optional)

Utensils

- 3 qt green mixing bowl
- pinch bowl
- measuring cup set
- silicone mixing spoon
- pastry brush
- rolling pin
- metal pie tin
- plastic wrap

Get Set!

1. In the green mixing bowl, combine the flour and shortening with 6–8 tablespoons of cold water to make a double pie crust, following the directions on page 42 and 43.
2. Separate into two discs, wrap in plastic and refrigerate for 15 minutes.
3. Combine the sugar and cinnamon in a pinch bowl.
4. Roll the chilled crust out into two circles. Place one in the pie tin.
5. Add the cherry pie filling, then top with the other crust. Pinch the edges together, then cut 6–8 slits in the crust to allow the steam to escape.
6. Use your pastry brush to apply a thin layer of water to the top crust.
7. Sprinkle the cinnamon and sugar mixture over the crust.

Get Cooking!

1. Bake the pie for 45–50 minutes or until the crust is nicely browned and the filling is bubbling.
2. Allow pie to cool.
3. Dig in and enjoy with a scoop of vanilla ice cream!

Get Creative!

Go Bananas!

There are so many ways to enjoy fresh bananas. Check out the recipes below for some simple and delicious ways to use bananas. What other ways can you think of to "go bananas?"

Banana Split

1. Split a banana lengthwise.
2. Top with three scoops of ice cream.
3. Drizzle with chocolate or strawberry ice cream topping.
4. Top with whipped cream, nuts, and put a cherry on top!

Peanut Butter Banana Quesadillas

1. Use the offset frosting spreader to apply a thin layer of peanut butter on a tortilla.
2. Arrange thin banana slices over half of the tortilla. Sprinkle chocolate chips over the banana slices and then fold the tortilla in half.
3. Cook the quesadilla in a skillet over medium-low heat until golden brown and crispy on both sides.

Chocolate Dipped Bananas

1. Cut bananas into 1-inch pieces.
2. Arrange on a wax paper-lined baking sheet and insert a toothpick into each piece.
3. Place bananas in freezer for 30 minutes or until firm.
4. Melt chocolate in the microwave or using a double-boiler.
5. Dip the banana pieces in the chocolate, then return to the tray.
6. Return to freezer until chocolate has hardened.

What Am I?

Test your knowledge of common cooking ingredients and utensils by using the clues below to answer the question: **What am I?**

I am a green member of the cabbage family that is named after the capitol of Belgium.

What am I? ____________________

I am made from an orchid and am used to add flavor to yogurt, ice cream, cookies, and cakes.

What am I? ____________________

I am shaped like a cylinder, have 2 handles, and am used to roll out dough.

What am I? ____________________

I have a round blade, a handle, and I come in handy when you are serving up a pizza.

What am I? ____________________

I have a handle with a wire bulb on the end, and I am a good tool to use when making scrambled eggs.

What am I? ____________________

I come from a cow and am used as a sweet and fluffy topping for pies, cupcakes, and ice cream sundaes.

What am I? ____________________

I am long and yellow, and you have to remove my peel before you can eat me.

What am I? ____________________

I am made from wheat and used to make bread, pie crust, and pasta.

What am I? ____________________

I am a healthy source of protein that comes from a bird you won't find in a tree.

What am I? ____________________

I grow on a tree that George Washington chopped down.

What am I? ____________________

Apple Pie Cake

SERVES:
12

PREP TIME:
40 minutes

READY TO EAT:
1 hour 20 minutes

Chefs-in-Training

What you'll learn:

- peeling apples
- coring apples
- measuring skills
- knife skills
- mixing skills

Shopping List

Got it!

- ○ apples (6)
- ○ eggs (3)
- ○ yellow cake mix (1 box)
- ○ brown sugar (1 ¾ cups)
- ○ flour (¾ cup)
- ○ butter (¾ cup)
- ○ half-and-half (½ cup)
- ○ oil (⅓ cup)
- ○ vanilla extract (1 T)
- ○ shortening (1 tsp)
- ○ cinnamon (1 tsp)
- ○ salt (½ tsp)
- ○ powdered sugar (2 T, optional)

Note to Grown Ups

The trickiest part of this recipe for young chefs is processing the apples. Peeling an apple can be a challenge with small hands, but the Curious Chef vegetable peeler has a safety guard so you can let your child give it a try, confident they will not hurt themselves. And the Curious Chef apple slicer makes coring and slicing apples an easy—and safe—one step process.

What's On Your Plate?

Write the ingredients that are part of a healthy plate where they belong on the organizer.

butter

eggs

apples

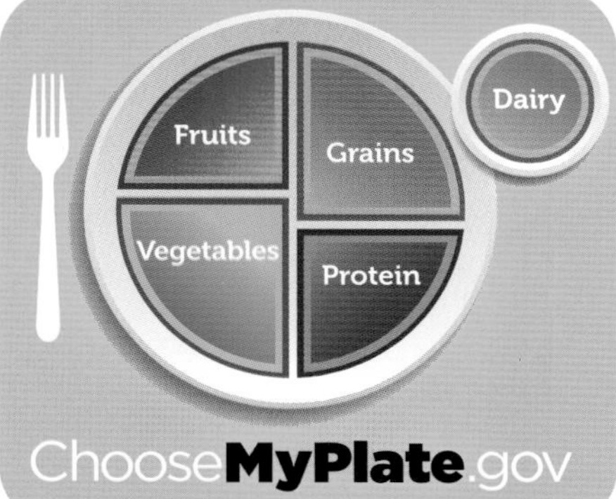

Cross out the ingredients that are not part of a healthy plate.

apples

cream

brown sugar

Which ingredient is a good source of fiber and vitamin C?

Which ingredients contain empty calories?

CURIOUS CHEF FOOD FACTS

Everyone knows apples grow on trees, but did you know the apple tree belongs to the rose family? An apple blossom is actually a kind of rose that produces the sweet, crisp fruit we call an apple.

Get Ready!

Ingredients

apples

eggs

yellow cake mix

brown sugar

butter

half-and-half

oil

flour

vanilla extract

cinnamon

salt

shortening

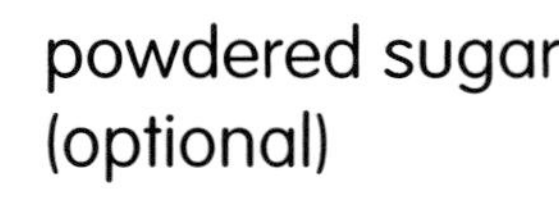

powdered sugar (optional)

Utensils

Cookware

- 9-x-13 cake pan

- saucepan (small)

Measurement

- measuring cup set

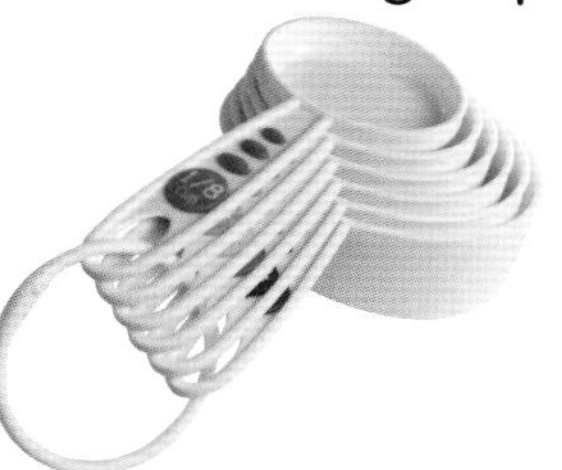

- measuring spoon set

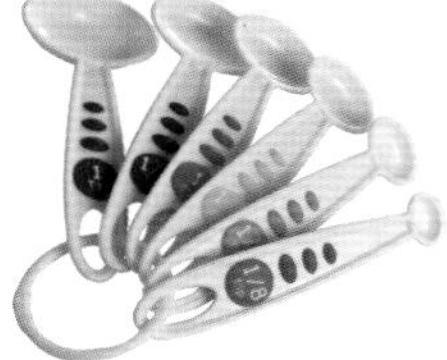

- clear measuring cup

Tools

- apple slicer

- nylon plastic knife

- poly spoon

- pastry blender or fork

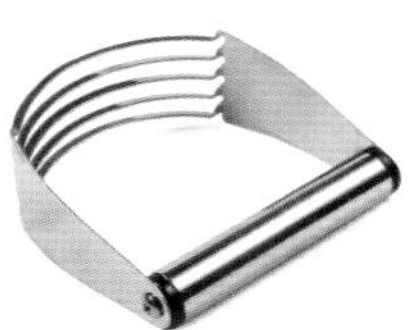

- vegetable peeler

- prep bowl set

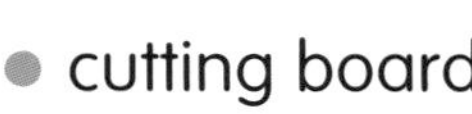

- cutting board

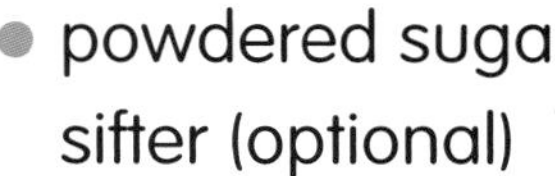

- powdered sugar sifter (optional)

Other

- mixing bowl set

Art Connection

Get creative with apples by cutting them in half—both from top to bottom and around the middle—inserting a wooden skewer into each half, then dipping them in different colored acrylic paints. Press the painted apple halves onto construction paper to create an apple-stamp masterpiece!

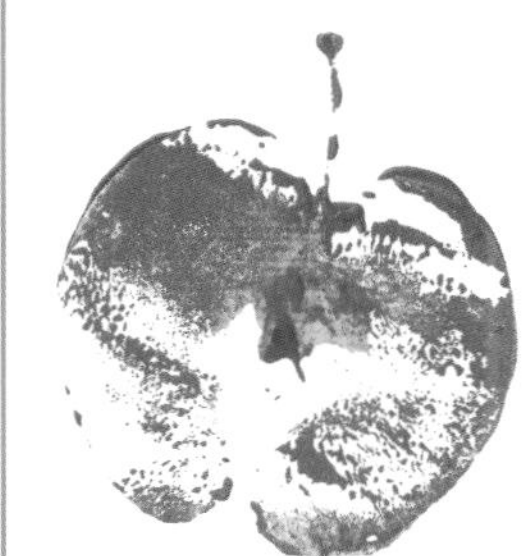

Get Set!

1 Prepare the cake pan.

- Grease the inside of the cake pan with a thin layer of shortening using a paper towel.
- Sprinkle a teaspoon or so of flour in the pan and shake the pan to spread the flour evenly over the bottom and up the sides of the pan.
- Hold the pan upside down over the sink and tap the bottom and sides to remove any loose flour.

2 Prepare the cake mix.

- In the green mixing bowl, measure and combine:
  - yellow cake mix
  - 3 eggs
  - ¾ cup water
  - ⅓ cup oil
- Stir briskly with the poly spoon for 2 minutes.
- Pour the batter into the cake pan.

3 Prepare the apples.

- Peel the apples using the fruit and vegetable peeler.
- Core and slice the apples using the apple slicer.
- Chop the apple slices.
- Add the apples to the orange mixing bowl, along with 3 tablespoons brown sugar and 1 teaspoon cinnamon. Toss to evenly coat the apple pieces.

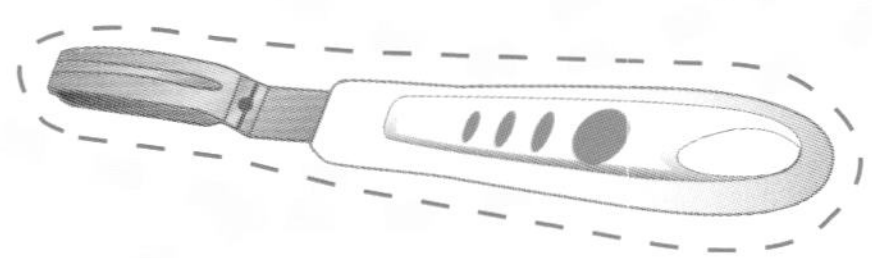

Make sure you take pictures as you go through the steps!

4 Make the topping.

- Cut ½ cup cold butter into ¼-inch square pieces.
- In the yellow mixing bowl, measure:
  - butter pieces
  - ¾ cup flour
  - ½ cup brown sugar
  - ¼ tsp salt
- Blend the ingredients using a pastry blender or fork until the butter is incorporated into the ingredients.

5 Assemble the cake.

- Spread the apple mixture over the cake batter.
- Sprinkle the topping evenly over the apples.

A Healthier You

Apples are one of the healthiest foods you can eat. They are high in fiber and vitamin C, and they have no fat and few calories. There are lots of ways to enjoy apples, including fresh, dried, stewed, and baked. Be a healthier you and find ways to include an apple a day in your diet.

Get Cooking!

1 Bake the cake.

- Bake the cake for about 35 minutes, then check for doneness by inserting a toothpick in the center of the cake.
- When the toothpick comes out clean, remove the cake and allow it to cool.

2 Prepare the caramel sauce.

- In the saucepan, measure and stir to combine:
  - 1 cup brown sugar
  - ½ cup half-and-half
  - ¼ cup butter
  - ¼ teaspoon salt

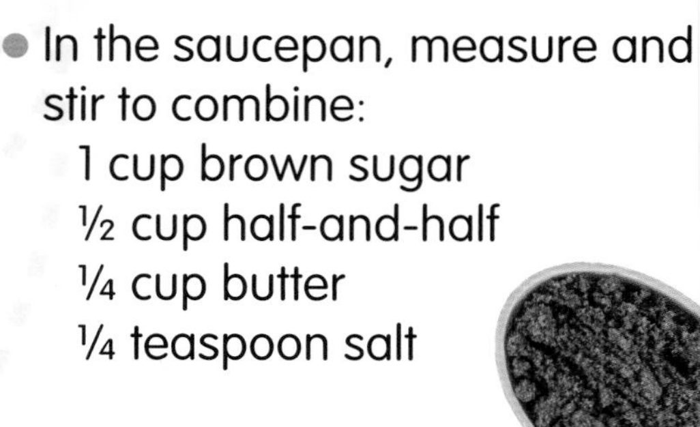

3 Cook the caramel sauce.

- Cook the sauce over medium-low heat, stirring gently for 5 to 7 minutes, until it starts to thicken.
- Add 1 tablespoon vanilla extract and cook another minute or until it is the consistency of syrup.
- Pour the sauce into the clear measuring cup to cool.

Make sure you take pictures as you go through the steps!

Finish the cake.

- When the cake is completely cooled, drizzle the caramel sauce in thin lines over the cake to make a pretty pattern.

Dig in and enjoy!

- For a special touch, use a powdered sugar sifter or spoon to apply a light dusting of powdered sugar.

Complete Your Meal

Dig in and enjoy with a scoop of vanilla ice cream or frozen yogurt!

Practice Makes Perfect!

Chicken Melon Salad

SERVES: 4

PREP TIME: 30 minutes 

READY TO EAT: 30 minutes 

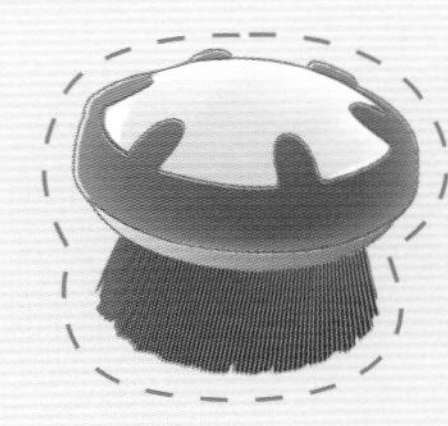

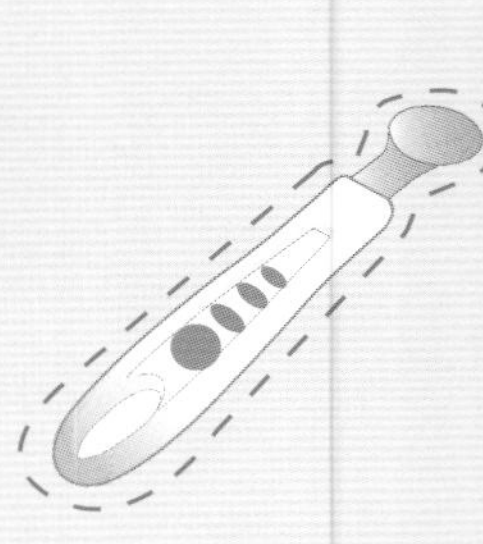

Get Ready!

Ingredients

- 1 ½ cups watermelon
- 1 ½ cups cantaloupe
- 1 lime
- 1 ⅓ lb rotisserie chicken
- 1 red onion
- ½ cup Gorgonzola cheese
- ½ cup walnuts or pecans
- 1 bunch basil
- ½ cup poppy seed salad dressing

Utensils

- melon baller
- measuring cup set
- large nylon plastic knife
- 3 qt green mixing bowl
- silicone mixing spatula
- prep bowl set
- cutting board

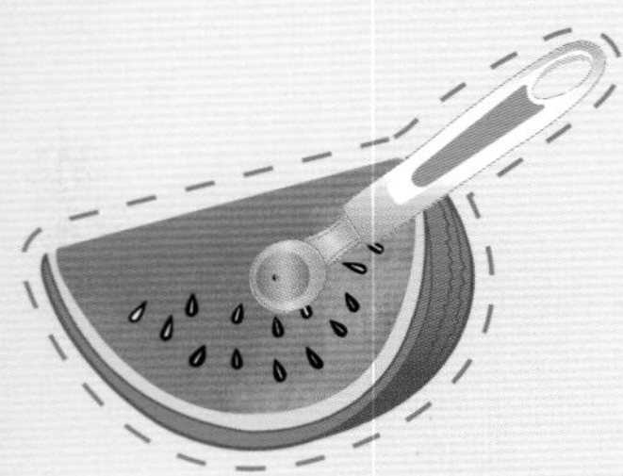

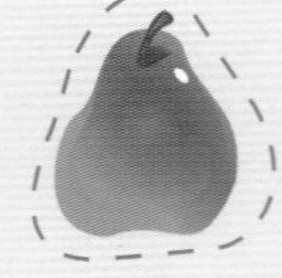

Get Set!

1. Cut the melons in half and use a spoon to remove all the seeds.
2. Use your melon baller to carve out balls of melon. Place in the green mixing bowl.
3. Peel and chop the red onion into small pieces. Add ¼ cup to the melon. Save any leftover onion pieces in an airtight container.
4. Crumble the Gorgonzola cheese into the green bowl.
5. Chop the basil into small, thin pieces. Add ¼ cup to the melon.
6. Squeeze the fresh lime juice into the green mixing bowl.
7. Chop the nuts into small pieces and add to the salad.
8. Chop the rotisserie chicken into small pieces and add to the salad.
9. Add the salad dressing and gently toss everything together using the silicone mixing spatula.
10. Dig in and enjoy garnished with a little more fresh basil!

Potato Pancakes

SERVES: 4–6

PREP TIME: 40 minutes 

READY TO EAT: 40 minutes 

Get Ready!

Ingredients

- 2 small zucchini, grated
- 1 carrot, grated
- 1 large potato, cooked and mashed
- ¼ cup flour
- 2 T oil
- ½ tsp thyme
- 2 tsp salt
- ¼ tsp pepper
- ¼ tsp baking powder
- sour cream (for topping)
- bacon bits (for topping)

Utensils

- 3 qt green mixing bowl
- 1 qt yellow mixing bowl
- colander
- whisk
- poly spoon
- measuring spoon set
- measuring cup set
- frying pan (large)
- cutting board

Get Set!

1. Place the grated zucchini in the colander and toss with 1 teaspoon salt. Set aside for at least 15 minutes.
2. Add the mashed potato, grated carrot, thyme, 1 teaspoon salt and pepper to the green mixing bowl.
3. In the yellow mixing bowl, whisk together the flour and baking powder. Add to the vegetable mixture.
4. Squeeze the water out of the zucchini using clean, washed hands. Add to the green bowl. Stir everything together with the poly spoon until the ingredients are well combined.
5. Form the mixture into lime-sized balls, then flatten into patties.

Get Cooking! 

1. Heat 2 tablespoons oil in the frying pan over medium heat. When the oil is hot, add the patties.
2. Cook the patties for 5–6 minutes on each side or until they turn golden brown.
3. Dig in and enjoy topped with a dollop of sour cream and a sprinkling of bacon bits!

Get Creative!

Apples Your Way

Apples can be enjoyed in all kinds of ways. Below are some quick and easy ways to turn plain old apples into delicious and healthy snacks and treats. Give these a try, then let your own creative juices flow and create a new way to eat this delicious fruit.

Stewed Applesauce

1. Peel, core, and chop 6 to 8 apples.
2. Place in a large saucepan with 2 tablespoons sugar, 1 teaspoon cinnamon, and 2–3 tablespoons water.
3. Stir to combine, then cover and cook over medium-low heat until apples are cooked through and very soft.
4. Blend in a blender to desired consistency.

Fresh Cinnamon Sugar Apples

1. Peel, core and chop apples into bite-sized pieces.
2. Toss with cinnamon and sugar.
3. Place in the refrigerator for 15–20 minutes to allow juices to sweat out.

My Creation

Baked Apple Crisp

1. Peel, core and dice 4 cups of apples.
2. Place in a 9-inch square baking dish.
3. Combine ¾ cup brown sugar, ½ cup flour, ½ cup old-fashioned oats, ⅓ cup butter, ½ tsp cinnamon, and ¼ tsp nutmeg.
4. Sprinkle the topping over the apples.
5. Bake at 375°F for 25–30 minutes or until apples are fork tender.

Have Some Fun!

A Fruit and Vegetable Rainbow

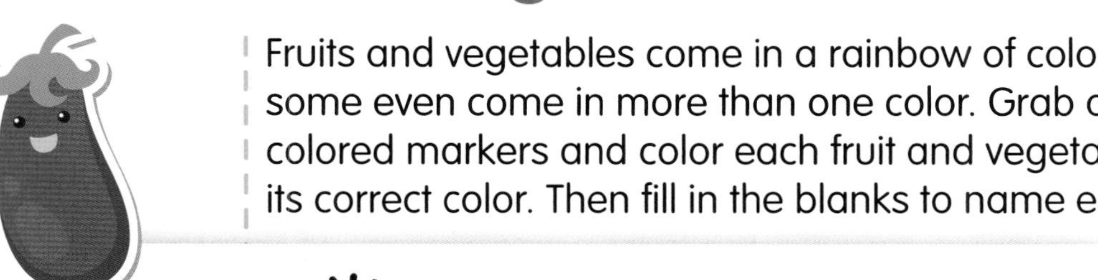

Fruits and vegetables come in a rainbow of colors, and some even come in more than one color. Grab a box of colored markers and color each fruit and vegetable below its correct color. Then fill in the blanks to name each item.

__ __ g g __ __ a n __

c __ __ n

__ i __ i

__ a __ a __ a

__ o __ __ __ o

__ r __ __ e __

Peanut Butter Whoopie Cookies

SERVES:
12 sandwiches

PREP TIME:
40 minutes

READY TO EAT:
1 hour 15 minutes

Chefs-in-Training

What you'll learn:

- measuring skills
- baking
- whisking
- cracking eggs
- melting chocolate

Shopping List

Got it!

- ○ quick cooking oatmeal (1 ½ cups)
- ○ peanut butter (1 ½ cups)
- ○ egg (1)
- ○ flour (½ cup)
- ○ sugar (½ cup)
- ○ butter (½ cup)
- ○ brown sugar (½ cup)
- ○ powdered sugar (½ cup)
- ○ baking powder (½ tsp)
- ○ baking soda (½ tsp)
- ○ salt (½ tsp)
- ○ vanilla extract (½ tsp)
- ○ baking chocolate (6 oz)

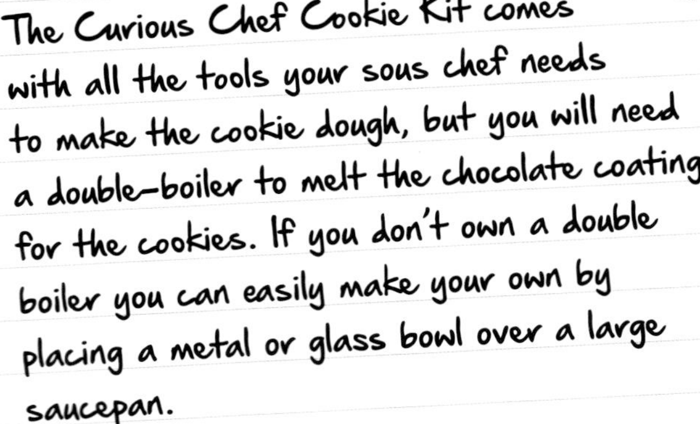

Note to Grown Ups

The Curious Chef Cookie Kit comes with all the tools your sous chef needs to make the cookie dough, but you will need a double-boiler to melt the chocolate coating for the cookies. If you don't own a double boiler you can easily make your own by placing a metal or glass bowl over a large saucepan.

What's On Your Plate?

Write the ingredients that are part of a healthy plate where they belong on the organizer.

butter

oatmeal

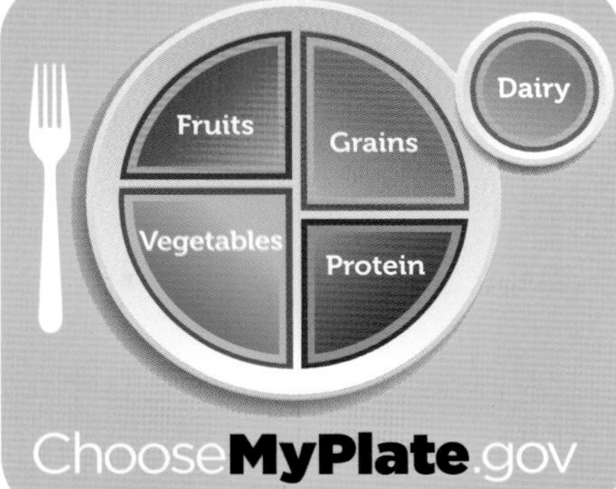

peanut butter

Cross out the ingredients that are not part of a healthy plate.

flour

sugar

peanut butter

Which ingredient is a whole-grain?

Which ingredient is both a source of protein and high in fat calories?

CURIOUS CHEF FOOD FACTS

What do chocolate and coffee have in common? More than you might think. Chocolate is made from cocoa beans which grow on the cacao tree. They look very much like coffee beans and are roasted much the same way. After roasting, the shells are removed and what's left is cocoa butter and chocolate solids, which are then turned into the final product we call chocolate.

Get Ready!

Ingredients

oatmeal

flour

sugar

brown sugar

baking powder

baking soda

salt

vanilla extract

peanut butter

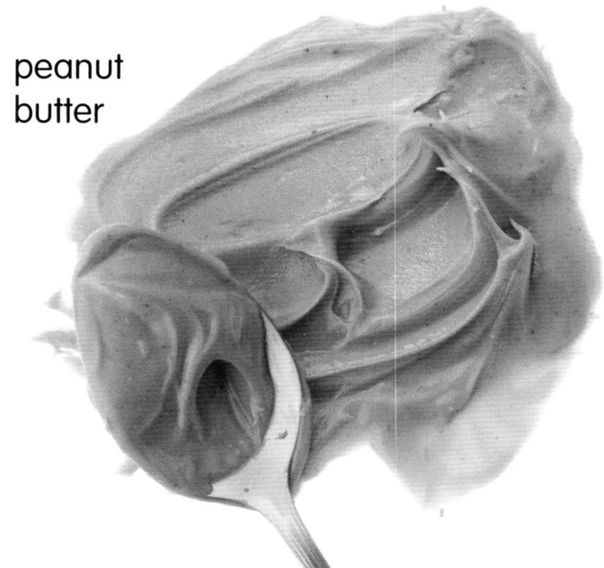

butter

egg

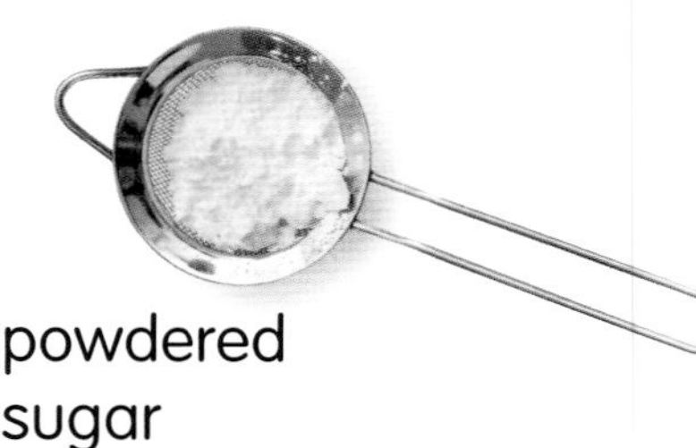
powdered sugar

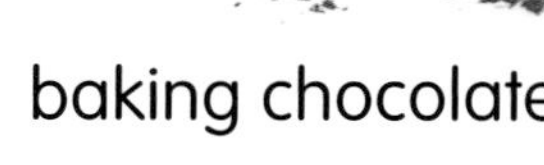
baking chocolate

Utensils

Cookware

- cookie sheet

- double boiler

Learning by Doing

You can make your own double boiler by placing a metal or glass bowl in a large saucepan.

Measurement

- measuring cup set

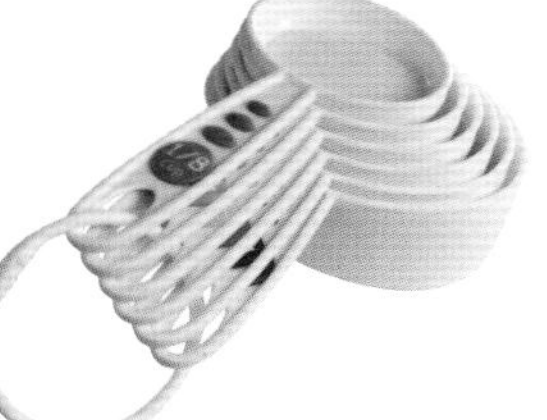

- measuring spoon set

Tools

- poly spoon
- cookie turner
- whisk

Other

- mixing bowl set

- prep bowl set

- wire cooling rack
- wax paper

Biology Connection

Did you know that peanuts aren't really nuts at all? That's right! They are actually part of the legume family and they don't grow on trees like other nuts, such as walnuts or almonds. The peanut plant is about 18-inches tall. It produces flowers above the ground, but the fruit of the plant—the peanuts—grow below ground in pods, similar to a pea or bean. Peanuts are planted in the spring and harvested in the fall and each plant produces about 40 pods with 2 to 3 peanuts in each pod.

Get Set!

1 Measure the dry ingredients.

- In the orange mixing bowl, measure:
  - 1 ½ cups oatmeal
  - ½ cup flour
  - ½ tsp baking powder
  - ½ tsp baking soda
  - ½ tsp salt
- Use your whisk to combine the ingredients.

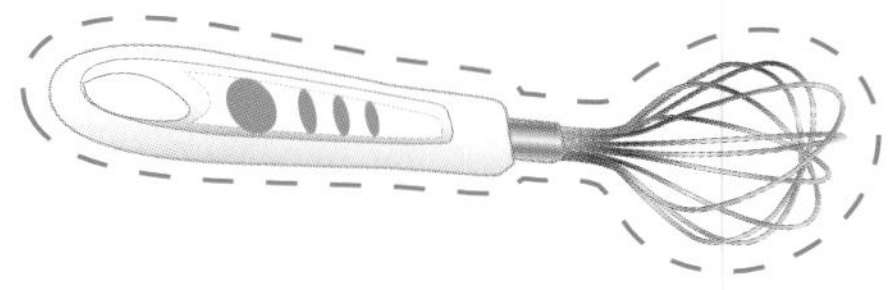

2 Blend the wet ingredients.

- In the green mixing bowl, measure and combine:
  - ½ cup (1 stick) softened butter
  - ½ cup sugar
  - ½ cup brown sugar
  - ½ cup peanut butter
  - 1 egg
  - ½ tsp vanilla extract
- Blend ingredients with the poly spoon until smooth.

3 Finish the cookie dough.

- Stir the oatmeal mixture into the peanut butter mixture a little bit at a time.
- Stir just until the ingredients are mixed together.
- Place rounded teaspoonfuls of batter on an ungreased baking sheet. Leave about an inch between each one.
- Use the tines of a fork to press dough down so they form small, flattened circles.

Make sure you take pictures as you go through the steps!

4 Make the filling.

- In the yellow mixing bowl, measure:
  ½ cup powdered sugar
  1 cup peanut butter
- Stir together with the poly spoon until it is light and fluffy. This may take about 5 minutes of mixing.

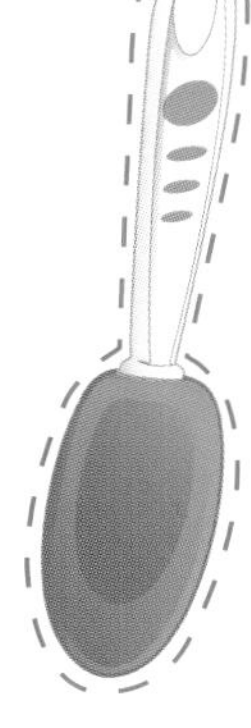

5 Prepare the double boiler.

- Fill the pan with about an inch of water.
- Place the insert or a bowl in the pan and make sure the bottom does not touch the water.

A Healthier You

Oatmeal is a whole grain that is a healthy addition to many baked goods because it adds fiber, protein, essential minerals, and carbohydrates to boost your energy. Be a healthier you and add oatmeal to all your favorite cookie and muffin recipes.

Get Cooking!

1 Bake the cookies.

- Bake the cookies for 8 minutes.
- Remove to a wire rack to cool completely.

2 Melt the chocolate.

- Heat the water in the double boiler over medium heat.
- Break the chocolate into squares and place it in the bowl.
- Stir as it begins to melt.
- When the chocolate is completely melted, turn the heat to the lowest setting to keep chocolate warm until you are ready to use it.

3 Assemble the sandwiches.

- Place half of the cooled cookies upside down on a flat surface.
- Stir the filling to lighten it up, then place a tablespoon in the center of each cookie.
- Place a second cookie on top, and gently squeeze the two halves together until the filling just starts to come to the edges.

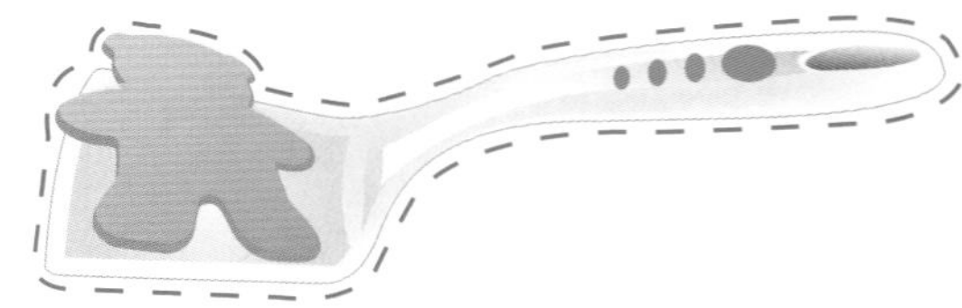

Make sure you take pictures as you go through the steps!

4 Dip the cookies.

- Pour the warm chocolate into a bowl.
- Dip each cookie sandwich about half way into the chocolate.
- Allow excess chocolate to drip back into bowl, then place the sandwiches on the cookie tray lined with wax paper.
- Place in the refrigerator to allow the chocolate to cool and set.

5 Dig in and enjoy!

Complete Your Meal

Dig in and enjoy your sandwich with a banana and a big glass of milk!

Practice Makes Perfect!

Fruit Pocket Cookies

SERVES: 8

PREP TIME: 15 minutes 

READY TO EAT: 1 hour 40 minutes  

Get Ready!

Ingredients

- 2 ¼ cups flour
- 1 jar jam or preserves
- ¾ cup butter, room temperature
- ⅔ cup sugar
- 1 egg, room temperature
- 1-5 tsp water (if needed)
- 1 tsp vanilla
- ¼ tsp salt
- fresh fruit

Utensils

- 3 qt green mixing bowl
- silicone mixing spoon
- measuring spoon set
- measuring cup set
- rolling pin
- cookie sheet
- flower cookie cutter
- prep bowl set
- plastic wrap
- parchment paper

Get Set!

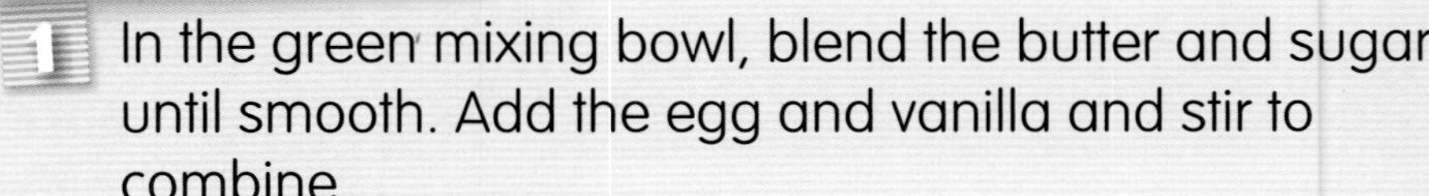

1. In the green mixing bowl, blend the butter and sugar until smooth. Add the egg and vanilla and stir to combine.
2. Add the flour and salt a little at a time and mix until a crumbly dough forms. Using your hands, knead the dough on a floured surface, adding water as necessary, until dough is firm enough to be rolled out and cut into shapes. Wrap in plastic and chill for about an hour.

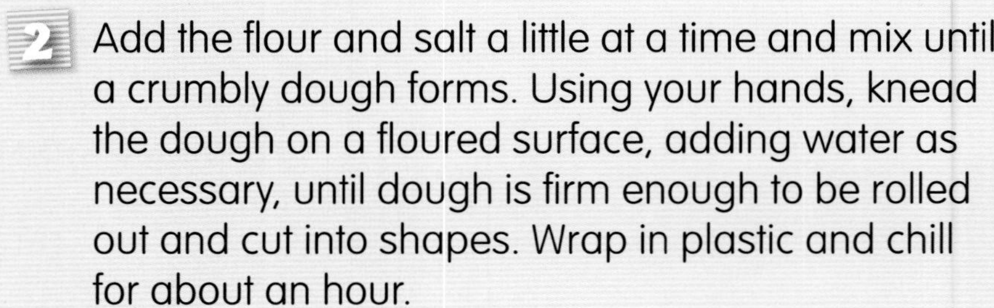

3. Roll the chilled dough out on a floured surface into an even, ⅛-inch thick layer.
4. Cut out cookies and transfer to a cookie sheet lined with parchment paper.
5. Place a teaspoon or so of jam in the center of each cookie.
6. Carefully fold up the "petals" to form a pocket to hold in the jam. Pinch the seams together as necessary to seal the cookies.

Get Cooking!

1. Bake the cookies at 350°F for 20 minutes or until edges start to brown. Remove to a wire rack to cool.
2. Dig in and enjoy with fresh fruit!

Double Chocolate Dream Cookies

SERVES: 8

PREP TIME: 15 minutes 

READY TO EAT: 1 hour 30 minutes 

Get Ready!

Ingredients

- 3 cups flour
- 2 eggs
- 1 ½ cups sugar
- 1 cup softened butter
- ⅔ cup unsweetened cocoa
- 1 tsp vanilla extract
- ½ tsp salt
- ½ tsp baking powder
- frozen vanilla yogurt (optional)
- strawberries (optional)

Utensils

- mixing bowl set
- poly spoon
- whisk
- rolling pin
- cookie cutter
- prep bowl set
- measuring spoon set
- measuring cup set
- plastic wrap

Get Set!

1. In the orange mixing bowl, whisk together the flour, salt, and baking powder.
2. In the yellow mixing bowl, blend the butter, sugar, eggs, vanilla and cocoa.
3. Gradually add the flour mixture to the butter mixture, stirring as you go until the mixture is smooth. Add a little water as needed. Wrap in plastic and chill for about an hour.
4. Roll chilled dough out on a floured surface to about ¼-inch thick. Cut out cookies with the cookie cutter. Use your cookie turner to transfer the cookies to a cookie tray lined with parchment paper.

Get Cooking!

1. Bake at 350°F for about 11 minutes or until the edges are firm and the centers are slightly soft and puffed.
2. Transfer to a wire rack to cool.
3. Dig in and enjoy with frozen vanilla yogurt and strawberries or a glass of milk!

Homemade Peanut Butter

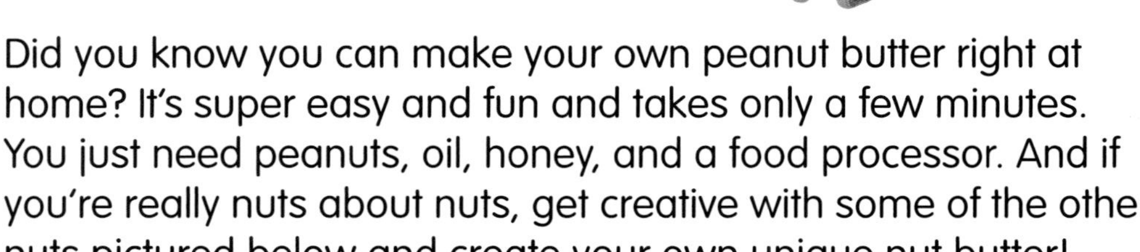

Did you know you can make your own peanut butter right at home? It's super easy and fun and takes only a few minutes. You just need peanuts, oil, honey, and a food processor. And if you're really nuts about nuts, get creative with some of the other nuts pictured below and create your own unique nut butter! How does chocolate-macadamia nut butter sound?

What You'll Need:

- 2 ½ cups Spanish peanuts
- 2 tablespoons honey
- 1 tablespoon peanut oil

What You'll Do:

1. Place the peanuts and honey into the bowl of a food processor.
2. Process for 1 minute or until the peanuts are finely chopped.
3. Scrape down the sides of the bowl and continue to process while slowly drizzling in the peanut oil.
4. Process another 1 to 2 minutes or until smooth, stopping now and then to scrape down the sides.

What's My Nickname?

Most of us call the main ingredient in peanut butter, peanuts. But in Georgia, where they grow lots and lots of peanuts, they have a special nickname for this tasty nut. Do you know what it is?

Write the name of each picture in the spaces next to it and the letters inside the box will reveal the answer.

What do Georgians call peanuts?

Italian Meatballs

SERVES:
6–8

PREP TIME:
30 minutes

READY TO EAT:
30 minutes

Chefs-in-Training

What you'll learn:

- measuring skills
- food safety
- testing for doneness
- cooking pasta

Shopping List

Got it!

- ○ spaghetti sauce (32-ounce jar)
- ○ ground beef (1 lb)
- ○ spaghetti noodles (1 lb)
- ○ ground pork (½ lb)
- ○ bread crumbs (½ cup)
- ○ Parmesan cheese (½ cup)
- ○ milk (1/3 cup)
- ○ egg (1)
- ○ salt (2 T)
- ○ olive oil (2 T)
- ○ Italian seasoning (1 ½ T)
- ○ garlic (2 cloves)

Note to Grown Ups

Few recipes are as much fun for kids to make as homemade meatballs because they can actually play with their food without getting in trouble for it! And it's a great recipe for practicing measuring skills. The bright color-coding and easy-to-pour shape of the Curious Chef measuring cups and spoons make measuring a snap for even the youngest chef-in-training.

What's On Your Plate?

Write the ingredients that are part of a healthy plate where they belong on the organizer.

milk

Parmesan cheese

eggs

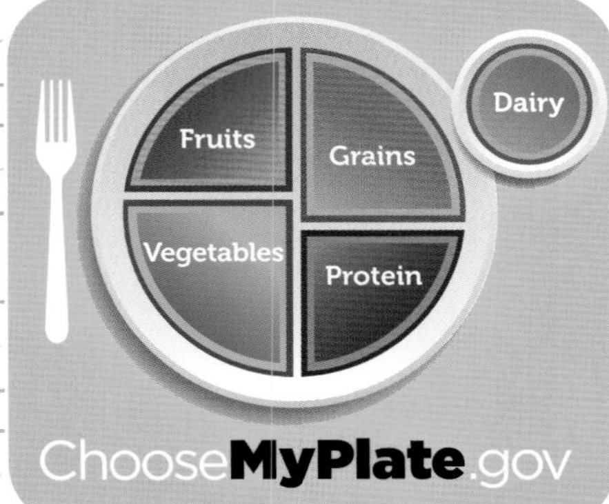

Cross out the ingredients that are not part of a healthy plate.

ground meat

spaghetti sauce

spaghetti

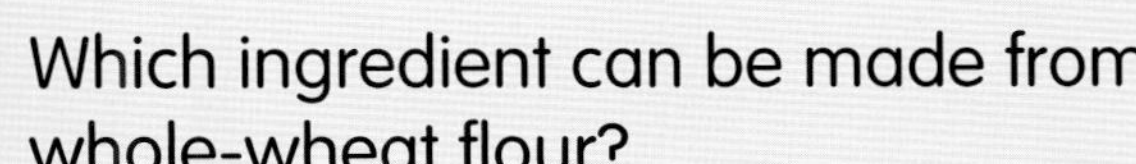

Which ingredient can be made from whole-wheat flour?

Which ingredients are a good source of both protein and calcium?

CURIOUS CHEF FOOD FACTS

One of the most commonly used ingredients in cooking is garlic. But is it an herb or spice? Actually it's neither. Herbs are green, spices are dried, so garlic is really considered a vegetable similar to onions, chives, and leeks.

Get Ready!

Ingredients

ground beef

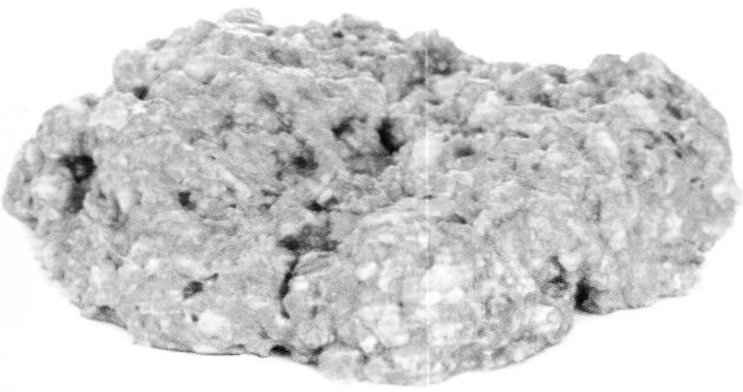

ground pork

bread crumbs

milk

Parmesan cheese

egg

Italian seasoning

garlic

spaghetti noodles

spaghetti sauce

salt

olive oil

Utensils

Cookware

- stock pot

- baking tray (large)

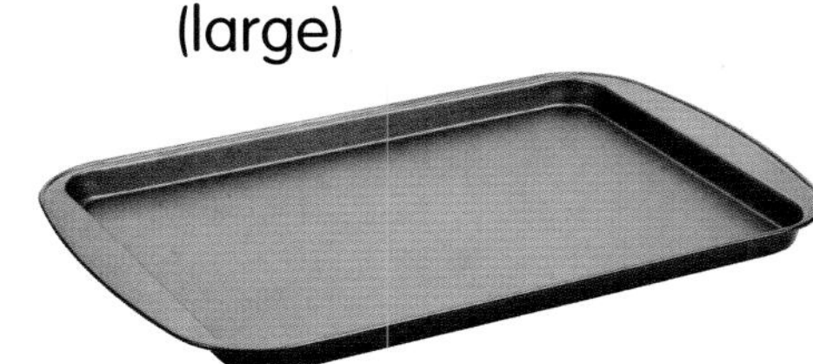

- skillet (large)

Measurement

- measuring cup set

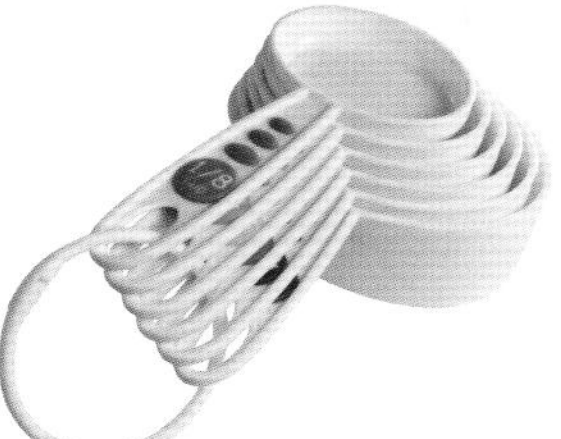

- measuring spoon set

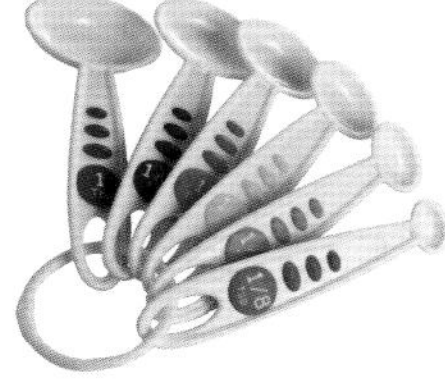

Tools

- nylon plastic knife
- serving tongs

- poly spoon

Other

- 3 qt green mixing bowl
- colander
- prep bowl set
- cutting board

Math Connection

One serving of meat (for an adult) is 3 ounces. This recipe uses 1 ½ pounds of meat to make 36 meatballs. How many meatballs are in one serving? (Use a calculator to find the answer.)

1 lb = 16 oz | ½ lb = ____ oz | 1 ½ lbs = 16 oz + ____ oz = ____ oz of meat

____ oz of meat ÷ 3 oz per serving = ____ total servings

36 meatballs ÷ ____ total servings = ____ meatballs per serving

There are about ____ meatballs in one serving.

Get Set!

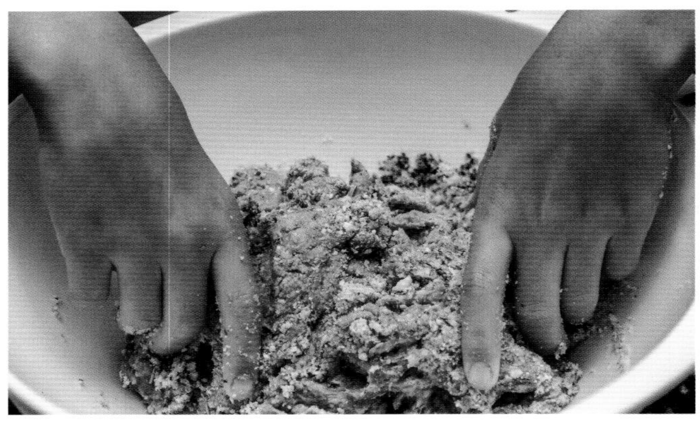

1 Make the meatballs.

- In the green mixing bowl, measure and then use your hands to mix together:
  - 1 lb ground beef
  - ½ lb ground pork
  - ½ cup dried breadcrumbs
  - ½ cup Parmesan cheese
  - 1 egg
  - 1 ½ T Italian seasoning
  - ⅓ cup milk
- Form into golf ball-sized meatballs and arrange on the baking tray, being sure to leave space between each meatball.
- Wash your hands thoroughly in warm, soapy water.

Learning by Doing

Wet your hands before rolling the meatballs to keep the meatball mixture from sticking to them.

2 Mince the garlic.

- Smash the cloves under the flat side of your nylon plastic knife.
- Remove the peel and mince the garlic into tiny pieces.

Learning by Doing

It may be difficult to mince the garlic with the nylon plastic knife. If so, either have your adult helper mince the garlic, or just put it in the sauce without mincing.

Make sure you take pictures as you go through the steps!

3 Prepare the spaghetti sauce.

- Pour the canned spaghetti sauce into the large skillet.
- Add the garlic to the sauce.

4 Prepare the pasta water.

- Fill the stock pot 2/3 full of water.
- Add 2 tablespoons salt, cover, and heat over high heat.

A Healthier You

Ground beef and pork are good sources of quality protein but can be high in fat and cholesterol. Be a healthier you and choose lean or extra-lean varieties, or try substituting with naturally lean white meats, such as ground chicken or turkey.

Get Cooking!

- Place the meatballs on the middle rack of the preheated oven.
- Bake uncovered for 15 minutes or until no longer pink inside.

1 Bake the meatballs.

- Cook the spaghetti in the stock pot according to the package directions.

2 Cook the pasta.

- Heat the spaghetti sauce over medium-low heat.

3 Heat the spaghetti sauce.

Make sure you take pictures as you go through the steps!

4 Finish the sauce.

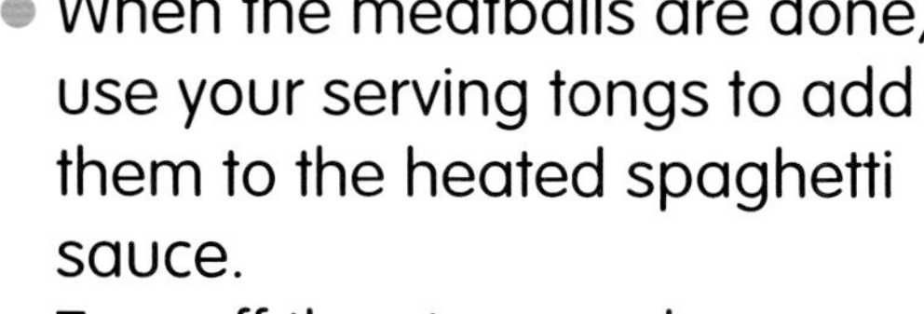

- When the meatballs are done, use your serving tongs to add them to the heated spaghetti sauce.
- Turn off the stove and cover the pan to keep the meatballs warm.

5 Drain the pasta.

- When the pasta is done, drain in the colander, then return to the stockpot.
- Toss with a little olive oil to keep the noodles from sticking together.

6 Dig in and enjoy!

- Top your spaghetti and meatballs with Parmesan cheese.

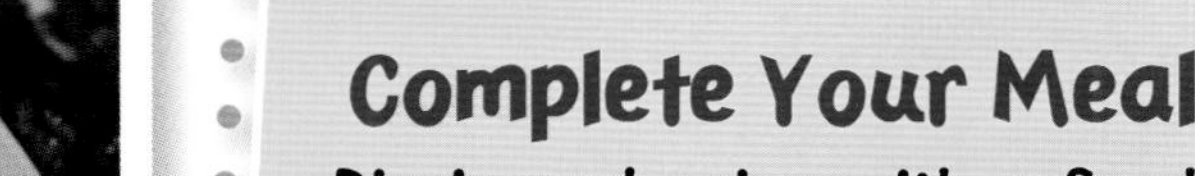

Complete Your Meal

Dig in and enjoy with a fresh green salad and garlic bread!

Practice Makes Perfect!

Cranberry Granola Bars

SERVES: makes 12 bars

PREP TIME: 15 minutes

READY TO EAT: 1 hour

Get Ready!

Ingredients

- 2 cups rolled oats
- 2 eggs
- ¾ cup flour
- ¾ cup dried cranberries
- ½ cup brown sugar
- ¼ cup oil
- ½ tsp vanilla extract
- ½ tsp salt
- ½ tsp cinnamon

Utensils

- 3 qt green mixing bowl
- measuring spoon set
- measuring cup set
- whisk
- silicone mixing spoon
- 8-inch square baking pan

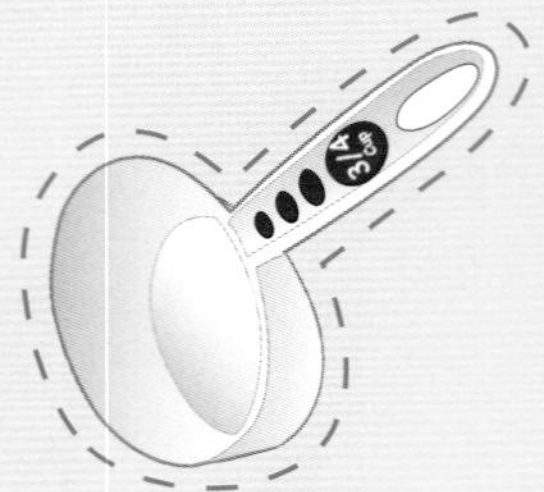

Get Set!

1. Crack the eggs into the green mixing bowl and whisk slightly. Then add the oil, vanilla, salt, and cinnamon. Stir to combine.
2. Add the oats, cranberries, flour and brown sugar to the egg mixture, and stir until smooth.
3. Grease the baking pan.
4. Spread the mixture in the baking pan using the back of your silicone mixing spoon to press it down firmly and evenly.

Get Cooking!

1. Set your timer for 30 minutes and bake the bars until they are cooked all the way through and lightly browned.
2. Let the bars cool completely in the pan before slicing.
3. Dig in and enjoy with a fruit smoothie or fresh sliced fruit!

Blueberry Croissant Puff

SERVES: 8

PREP TIME: 10 minutes 

READY TO EAT: 1 hour 10 minutes 

Get Ready!

Ingredients

- 3 large croissants
- 2 eggs
- 1 cup milk
- 1 cup fresh blueberries
- 8 oz cream cheese, softened
- 2/3 cup sugar
- 1 tsp vanilla extract
- 2 T powdered sugar (optional)

Utensils

- 3 qt green mixing bowl
- 9-in square casserole dish
- measuring spoon set
- measuring cup set
- clear measuring cup
- poly spoon
- powdered sugar sifter (optional)

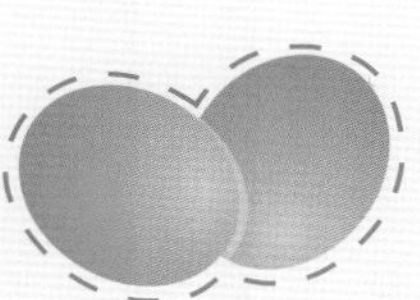

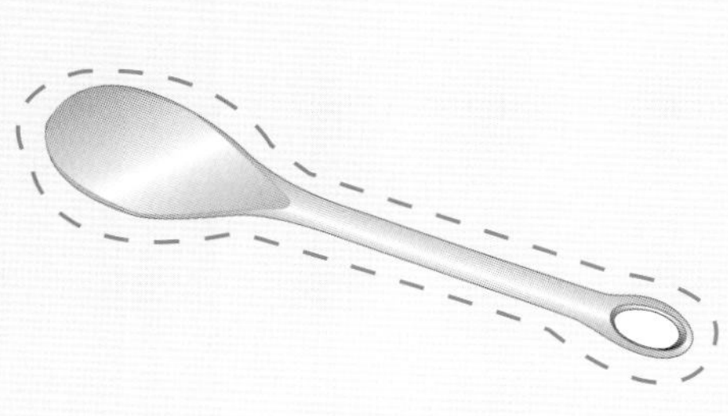

Get Set!

350° Pre-heat

1. Break croissants into small pieces. Place in casserole dish.
2. Sprinkle with blueberries.
3. Stir cream cheese, sugar, eggs, and vanilla with your poly spoon until thoroughly combined.
4. Gradually pour in the milk and stir until thoroughly combined. Pour over the croissant pieces. Let stand 20 minutes or overnight.

Get Cooking!

1. Bake at 350°F for 35–40 minutes or until set in the center and golden brown.
2. Cover with foil for the last 10 minutes if the top is getting too brown.
3. Dig in and enjoy warm and sprinkled with a light dusting of powdered sugar.

Get Creative!

Meatless Veggie Balls

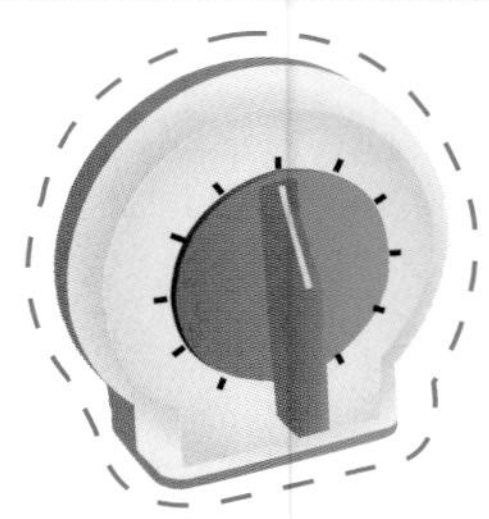

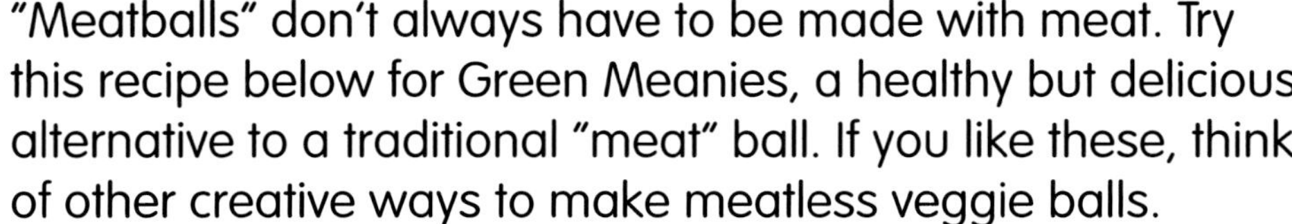

"Meatballs" don't always have to be made with meat. Try this recipe below for Green Meanies, a healthy but delicious alternative to a traditional "meat" ball. If you like these, think of other creative ways to make meatless veggie balls.

Green Meanies

What You'll Need:

- 20-oz frozen spinach (thawed and thoroughly drained)
- 1 box stuffing mix (chicken flavor)
- 1 cup Parmesan cheese
- 5 eggs (lightly whisked)
- 1 onion (finely minced, or grated)
- ½ cup butter (melted)
- 1 T oregano
- 1 T basil
- 2 cloves garlic (crushed)
- 8 oz mozzarella cheese (finely grated)

What You'll Do:

1. Lightly whisk the eggs in the green mixing bowl.
2. Add the remaining ingredients and mix together until the spinach is evenly distributed throughout the other ingredients.
3. Form into small balls.
4. Arrange on a large greased baking tray and bake at 350°F for 15 minutes.
5. Eat warm. Freeze any leftovers and reheat in the microwave for a quick and delicious power snack!

Have Some Fun!

Crossword Puzzle

Across

1. Something you wear to keep your clothes clean while cooking.

7. Something you would use to boil water.

8. Something you should never use without permission from an adult.

11. Something you use to protect your countertop when slicing an onion.

12. Something you use to make sure you don't cook something too long.

Down

2. Something you would use when making a pie crust.

3. A good tool for beating eggs.

4. Something you would use to bake a cake.

5. A good tool to use to drain spaghetti.

6. What you do when you want an exact amount of something.

9. Something you would use to stir things.

10. Something you should always use when handling hot things.

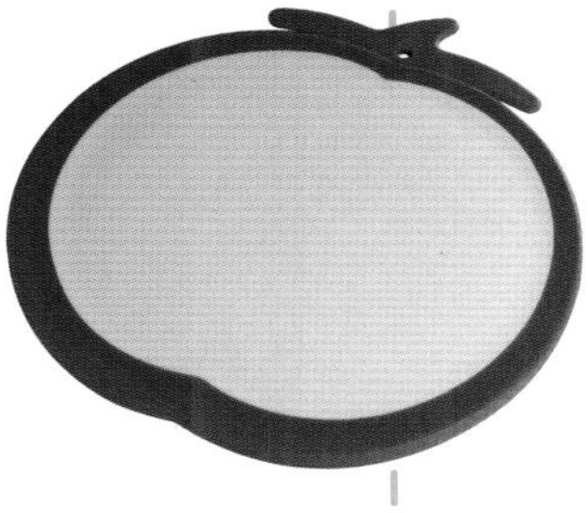

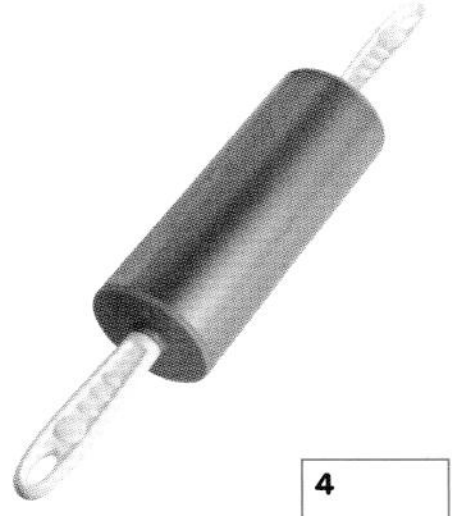

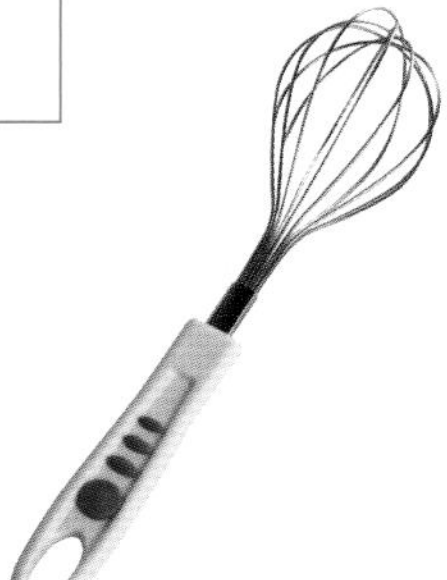

French Toast Pops

SERVES:
2–4

PREP TIME:
20 minutes

READY TO EAT:
20 minutes

Chefs-in-Training

What you'll learn:

- cracking eggs
- whisking eggs
- measuring skills
- pan frying
- using cookie cutters

Shopping List

Got it!

- ○ sliced bread (4 slices)*
- ○ eggs (3)
- ○ milk or cream (¼ cup)
- ○ butter (2 T)
- ○ powdered sugar (2 T)
- ○ sugar (1 T)
- ○ cinnamon (1 tsp)
- ○ vanilla extract (¼ tsp)
- ○ syrup (for dipping)
- ○ wooden skewers (4)

* Make sure to buy a loaf of bread that is bigger than the flower cookie cutter.

Note to Grown Ups

The only thing better than French toast is French toast on a stick! This is a foolproof recipe that budding chef's can prepare all on their own. Measuring liquids is a snap with the Curious Chef 2-cup clear measuring cup with its child-friendly handle, colorfully coded measurements for easy reading and three pour spouts for no-mess pouring. What a delicious way to learn such a useful skill!

Pink Chef's Kit

What's On Your Plate?

Write the ingredients that are part of a healthy plate where they belong on the organizer.

butter

milk

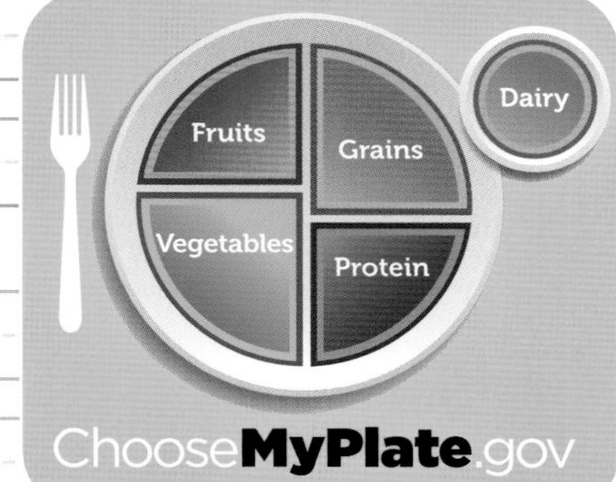

bread

Cross out the ingredients that are not part of a healthy plate.

bread

eggs

sugar

What could you serve with your French toast pops to make it a more complete healthy plate?

What kind of bread could you use in order to make this meal healthier?

CURIOUS CHEF FOOD FACTS

Everyone knows vanilla is used to flavor ice cream, cakes, and frosting, but it has many more uses than that. Vanilla is used in medicines to make them taste good and as a fragrance to hide the smell of stinky things like rubber tires, paint and cleaning products. And, if spiders give you the creeps, you can use whole vanilla beans to scare them away because spiders don't like the smell!

Get Ready!

Ingredients

bread

eggs

milk or cream

sugar

butter

vanilla extract

powdered sugar

cinnamon

syrup

Utensils

Cookware

- pancake griddle

Measurement

- measuring spoon set

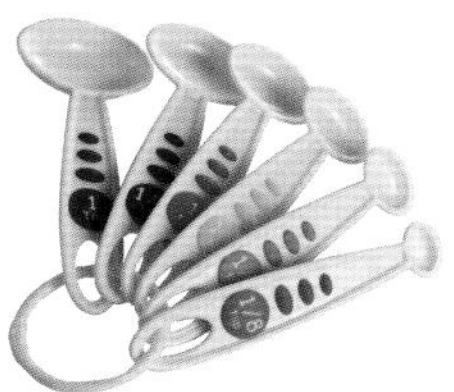

- clear measuring cup

Tools

- whisk

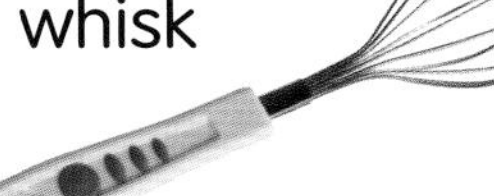

- cutting board

- cookie cutter

- powdered sugar sifter

Other

- 1 qt yellow mixing bowl

- ice cream bowls (for dipping)

- wooden skewers (4)

History Connection

In France, French toast is often called pain perdu, or "lost bread." They considered it "lost" when it went stale and became too dried out to eat. But centuries ago, poor French families couldn't afford to throw it out so they soaked the stale bread in eggs and milk to soften it up, fried it in butter, and voilà—French toast was born!

Get Set!

1 Prepare the eggs.

- Crack 3 eggs into the yellow mixing bowl.
- Whisk the eggs until they are thoroughly combined.

Learning by Doing

"Thoroughly combined" means there is no sign of gooey egg white or yellow egg yolk.

2 Measure the milk or cream.

- Measure ¼ cup milk or cream and add it to the eggs.

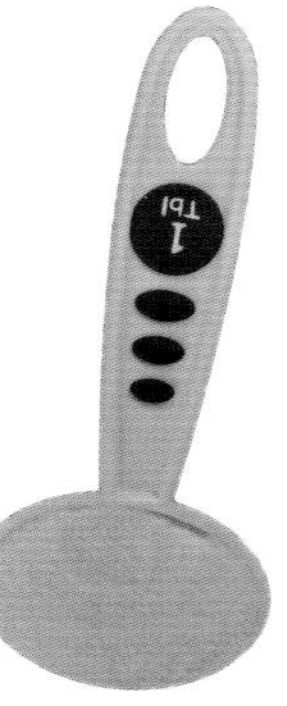

3 Measure the flavorings.

- To the eggs, measure and add:
  - 1 tablespoon sugar
  - 1 teaspoon cinnamon
  - ¼ teaspoon vanilla extract

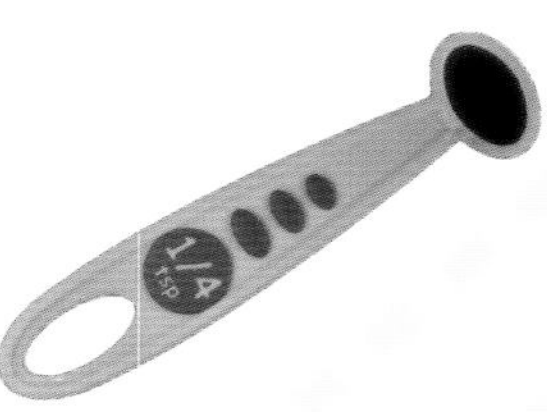

Make sure you take pictures as you go through the steps!

4 Whisk the egg mixture.

- Whisk the egg mixture again until all ingredients are thoroughly combined.

5 Prepare the bread.

- Use the flower cookie cutter to cut out flowers from 4 slices of bread.
- Insert a wooden skewer into the center of each flower cut out.

A Healthier You

French bread is made from refined white flour, not whole-grain flour. Refined grains have had the bran and germ removed, which also removes heart-healthy fiber, iron, and many B vitamins. Be a healthier you and make sure half the grains you eat are whole grains.

Get Cooking!

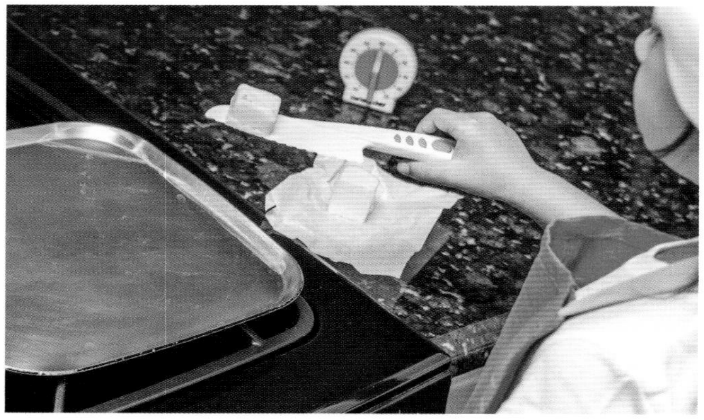

1 Prepare the pan.

- Preheat the skillet or griddle over medium heat for about 5 minutes.
- When the pan is hot, add 1 tablespoon butter.

Learning by Doing

Butter burns easily and quickly if the pan is too hot. When cooking with butter, cook food slowly over medium heat to avoid burning.

2 Soak the bread.

- One at a time, soak both sides of the bread cut outs in the egg mixture by tilting the bowl slightly.

Learning by Doing

Spoon the egg mixture over the bread if necessary to get it completely soaked with the mixture.

3 Cook the bread.

- Place the bread slices in the pan and cook for 3–4 minutes or until it turns golden brown.
- Flip the bread over and cook the other side until it turns golden brown.
- Remove to a serving plate.

Make sure you take pictures as you go through the steps!

4 Top with powdered sugar.

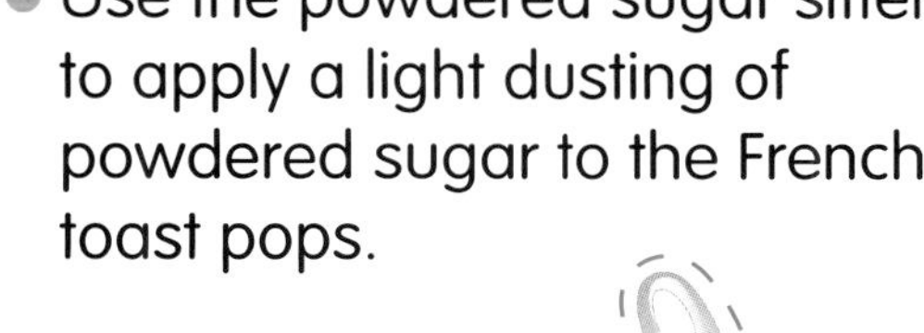

- Use the powdered sugar sifter to apply a light dusting of powdered sugar to the French toast pops.

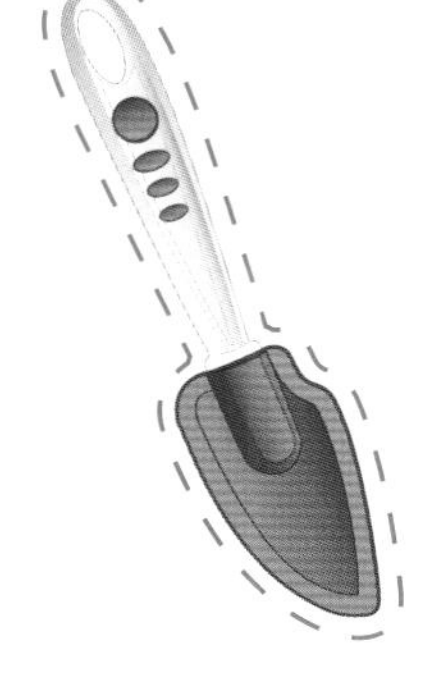

5 Dig in and enjoy!

- Pour syrup into the ice cream bowls for dipping.

Complete Your Meal

Dig in and enjoy with fresh fruit and bacon or sausage.

Practice Makes Perfect!

Basic White Bread

SERVES: 6–8 | PREP TIME: 20 minutes  | READY TO EAT: 2 1/2 hours 

Get Ready!

Ingredients

- 3 ½ cups bread flour
- 1–1 ⅛ cups warm water
- ¼ oz package fast-acting dried yeast
- 1 tsp salt
- 1 tsp sugar
- milk (for brushing)
- cooking spray

Utensils

- 3 qt green mixing bowl
- poly spoon
- loaf pan
- pastry brush
- wire cooling rack
- measuring spoon set
- measuring cup set
- clear measuring cup

Get Set!

425° Pre-heat

1. Combine the flour, salt, sugar, and yeast in the green mixing bowl. Make a well in the center and pour in 1 cup warm water.
2. Use your poly spoon to combine the water and flour, then use your hands to mix until a smooth dough forms. Add more water (for remaining ⅛ cup as needed) to make the dough stick together. Form the dough into a ball.
3. On a floured surface, knead the dough for 5 minutes.
4. Put the dough in the bowl, cover it with a damp towel, and leave it in a warm place for an hour, or until it has doubled in size.
5. Punch the risen dough to "deflate" it, then knead it 5–10 more times.

Get Cooking!

1. Place the dough in a greased baking pan.
2. Use your pastry brush to apply a light coating of milk to the top of the loaf.
3. Bake for about 30 minutes or until it turns light golden brown.
4. Place on a wire rack to cool.
5. Dig in and enjoy with jam or your favorite lunch meat!

Welsh Cakes

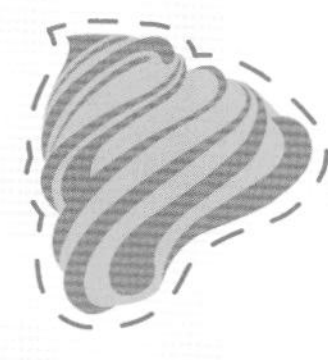

SERVES: 4–6

PREP TIME: 15 minutes

READY TO EAT: 15 minutes

Get Ready!

Ingredients

- 1 ¾ cups self-rising flour
- ½ cup butter (softened)
- ¼ cup sugar
- ¼ cup dried cranberries
- 1 egg
- 2 T milk
- 2 T oil
- ½ tsp salt

Utensils

- 3 qt green mixing bowl
- measuring spoon set
- measuring cup set
- poly spoon
- rolling pin
- flower cookie cutter or round glass
- pancake griddle
- cookie turner

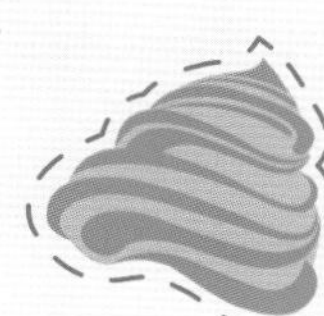

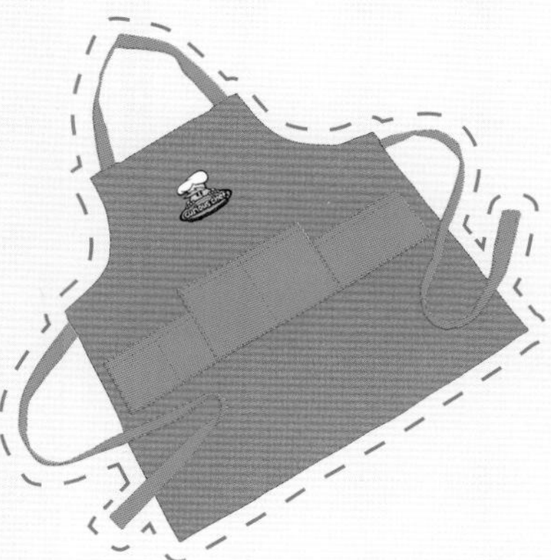

Get Set!

1. In the green mixing bowl, stir together the flour, salt, butter, sugar and dried cranberries.
2. Add the egg and milk and mix together until a fairly stiff dough forms.
3. Roll the dough out on a floured surface into an even ¼-inch thick sheet.
4. Cut out as many biscuits as you can, then gather up the trimmings, roll out the dough, and cut out more biscuits.

Get Cooking!

1. Heat the griddle over medium-high heat. Add enough oil to coat the surface of the griddle.
2. When the oil is hot, cook the biscuits for about 3 minutes on each side.
3. Coat the hot Welsh cakes on both sides with sugar.
4. Dig in and enjoy warm or cold with a pad of butter!

Get Creative!

Cookie Cutter Bird Feed Cakes

There's nothing like a bird feed cake to get birds of all kinds of feathers to flock together—right in your own backyard! Making a homemade bird feed cake for your backyard is a fun and creative way to help feed our feathered friends and to get to see them a little better.

What You'll Need:

- ¾ cup birdseed
- ¼ cup water
- 1 small envelope of gelatin
- twine or string
- cookie cutters
- drinking straw
- wax paper

What You'll Do:

1. Combine the gelatin with ¼ cup of water and bring to a simmer while stirring.
2. Continue stirring until the gelatin is completely dissolved.
3. Remove from heat and let cool for a minute.
4. Stir in the birdseed.
5. Arrange your cookie cutters out on wax paper and fill with the birdseed mixture.
6. To create a hanging string hole, insert a straw into the birdseed mixture.
7. Pack the mixture firmly and tightly into the cookie cutters and around the straw, just like when you are measuring brown sugar.

Learning by Doing

If you don't pack the mixture in tightly enough the feeders will fall apart when you remove the cookie cutter.

8. Allow the mixture to dry overnight.
9. Remove from the cookie cutters. Carefully remove the straws and insert twine through the hole to form a loop for hanging.
10. Hang near a window and then watch as the birds in backyard enjoy their new treat!

Where Does This Come From?

Everything we eat comes from either plants or animals. But have you ever wondered which plant or animal the foods you eat come from? Look at the pictures of the raw food items below and then draw a line to match the raw item with the food product that is made from it.

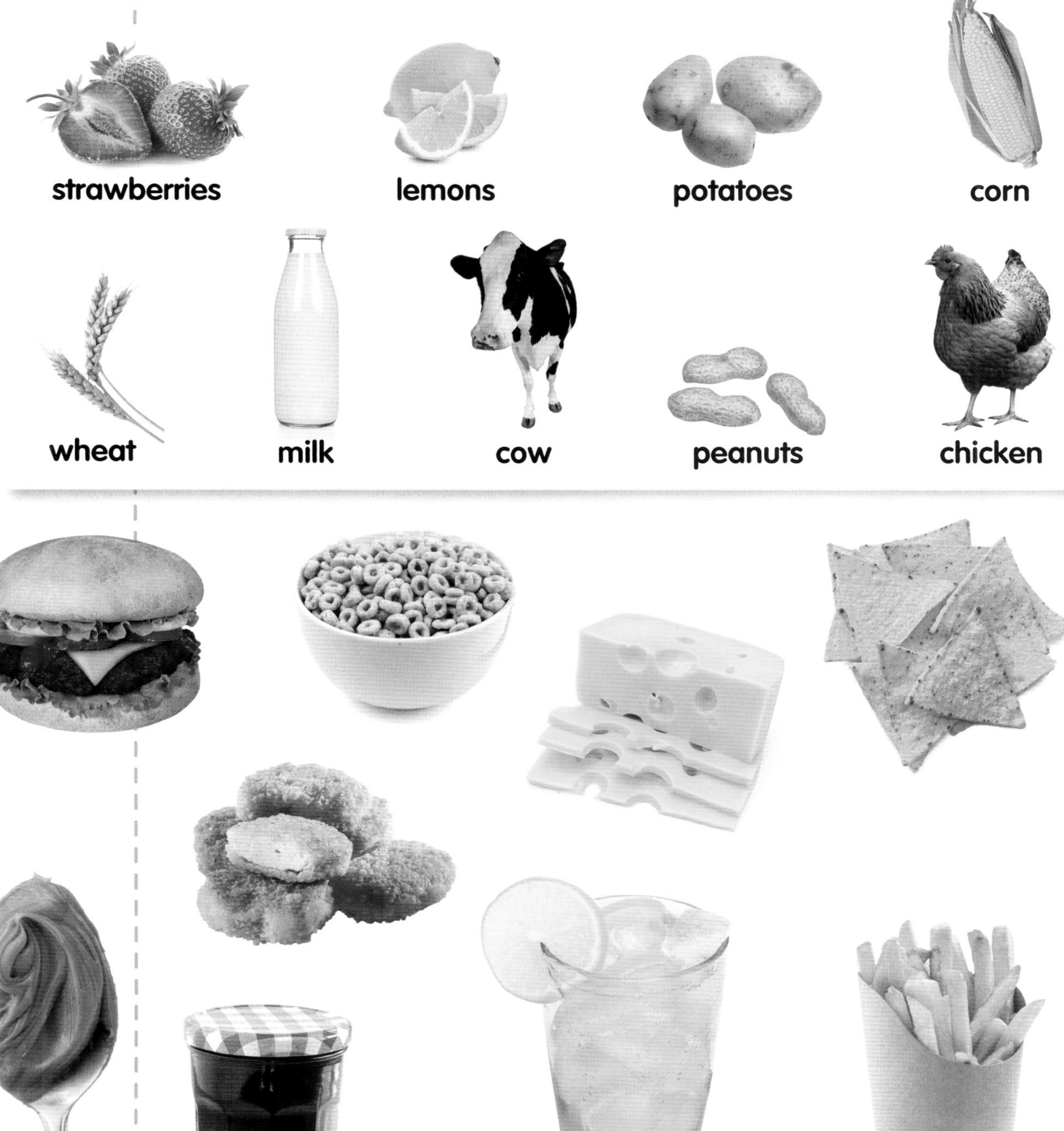

Chocolate Zucchini Muffins

SERVES:
6 muffins

PREP TIME:
30 minutes

READY TO EAT:
1 hour

Chefs-in-Training

What you'll learn:

- measuring skills
- mixing skills
- grating skills
- cracking eggs
- making frosting

Shopping List

Got it!

- flour (1 cup)
- milk (2/3 cup)
- heavy cream (1 cup)
- eggs (1 large)
- zucchini (1 small)
- chocolate chips (½ cup)
- dark chocolate (8 ounces)
- brown sugar (1/3 cup)
- unsweetened cocoa powder (¼ cup)
- vegetable oil (2 T)
- baking powder (2 tsp)
- vanilla extract (1 tsp)
- salt (¼ tsp)

Note to Grown Ups

Zucchini in a chocolate muffin may sound strange at first, but when you taste these chocolate delights, you may forget that they are actually good for you. Your sous chef should be able to grate the zucchini with little help, but baking chocolate is very hard so you may want to complete this step for them.

chocolate

What's On Your Plate?

Write the ingredients that are part of a healthy plate where they belong on the organizer.

milk

eggs

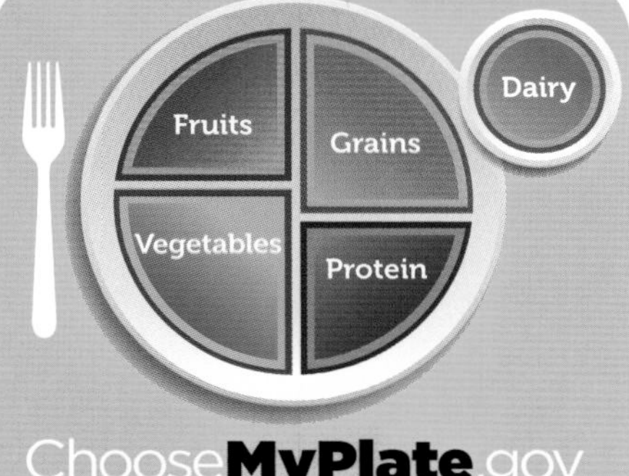

zucchini

zucchini

Cross out the ingredients that are not part of a healthy plate.

heavy cream

brown sugar

flour

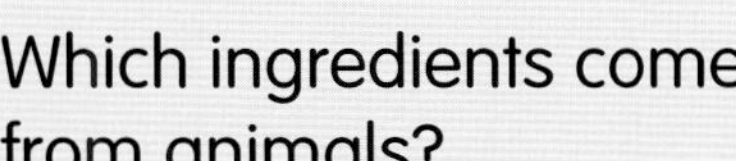

Which ingredients come from animals?

Which contains less fat, milk or cream?

Curious Chef Food Facts

Dark chocolate is full of nutrients that are actually good for you. It contains less sugar than milk chocolate (the kind used in candy bars), and it contains antioxidants, fiber, and minerals that can positively affect your health.

Get Ready!

Ingredients

flour

milk

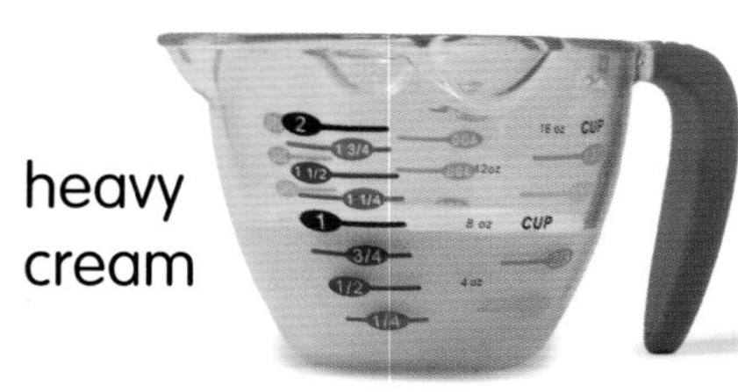

heavy cream

egg

zucchini

chocolate chips

dark chocolate

brown sugar

unsweetened cocoa powder

vegetable oil

baking powder

vanilla extract

salt

Utensils

Cookware

- muffin tin

- saucepan (small)

Measurement

- measuring spoon set

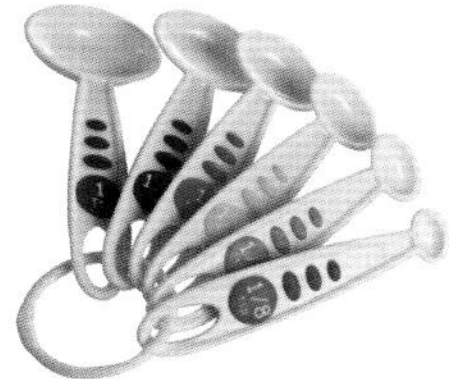

- measuring cup set

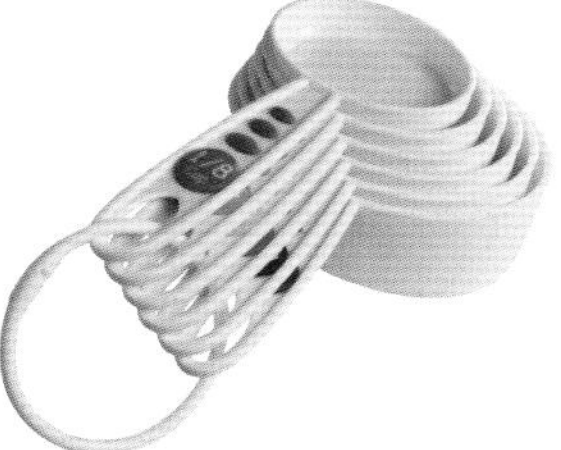

- clear measuring cup

Tools

- poly spoon
- nylon plastic knife
- silicone mixing spoon

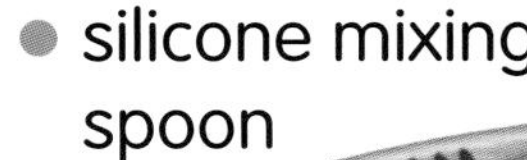

- cheese grater

- whisk

- offset frosting spreader

Other

- mixing bowl set

- silicone cupcake liners
- prep bowl set

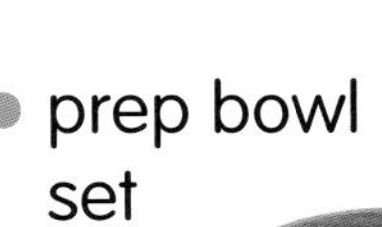

- cutting board

Math Connection

Do you know what 1 minus $\frac{1}{3}$ is? You can use your measuring tools to find the answer.

1. Fill the clear measuring cup to the 1-cup mark.
2. "Subtract" $\frac{1}{3}$ by pouring out $\frac{1}{3}$ cup into the $\frac{1}{3}$ measuring cup.

How much is left in the clear measuring cup?

_____ cup

$1 - \frac{1}{3} =$ _____

Use your measuring cups to solve these other fraction problems.

$\frac{1}{2} - \frac{1}{4} =$ _____

$1 - \frac{2}{3} =$ _____

$2 - \frac{1}{2} =$ _____

$1\frac{1}{2} - \frac{3}{4} =$ _____

Get Set!

1 Mix the wet ingredients. 425° Pre-heat

- In the green mixing bowl, measure and whisk together until smooth:
  - 1/3 cup firmly packed brown sugar
  - 2 tablespoons vegetable oil
  - 1 egg
  - 1/3 cup milk
  - 1 teaspoon vanilla extract

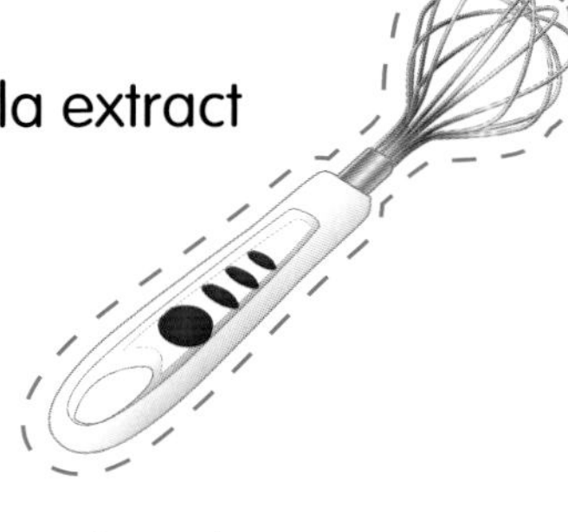

2 Mix the dry ingredients.

- In the orange mixing bowl, measure and whisk together:
  - 1 cup flour
  - 1/4 cup unsweetened cocoa powder
  - 2 teaspoons baking powder
  - 1/4 teaspoon salt

3 Mix the batter.

- Gently fold the flour mixture into the wet mixture using your silicone mixing spoon. (The batter will be thick!)

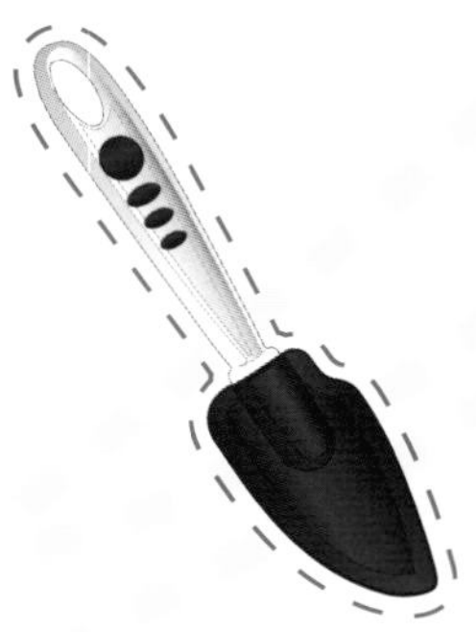

Grate the zucchini.

- Use a cheese grater to grate the zucchini.

Finish the batter.

- Add the grated zucchini and ½ cup chocolate chips to the batter.
- Stir the mixture just until the ingredients are thoroughly combined.

6 Prepare the muffin tin.

- Place the silicone cupcake liners in the muffin tin.
- Divide the batter evenly among the muffin cups.

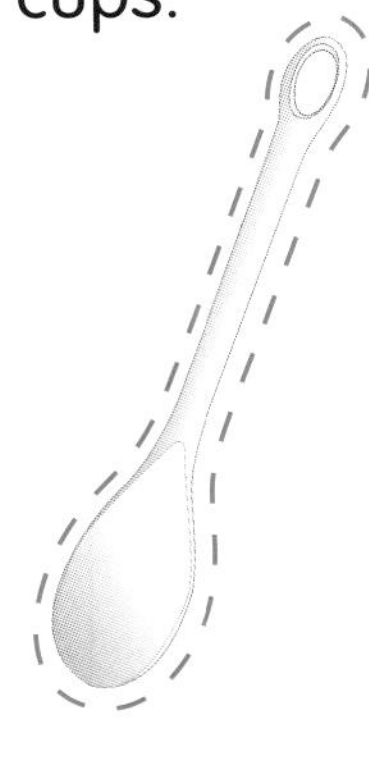

Get Cooking!

1 Bake the muffins.

- Bake the muffins at 425°F for 5 minutes.
- Reduce the heat to 375°F and continue baking an additional 15 minutes, or until a toothpick inserted in a muffin comes out clean.

Be sure to set a timer for 5 minutes so the muffins don't burn.

2 Grate the dark chocolate.

- Grate 8 ounces dark chocolate.
- Place in the orange mixing bowl.

3 Heat the heavy cream.

- In a small saucepan, bring 1 cup heavy cream to a boil over medium-high heat.
- As soon as it begins to boil, pour it into the bowl with the chocolate.

Make sure you take pictures as you go through the steps!

4 Finish the frosting.

- Stir the cream until the chocolate melts.
- Set it aside for 5 minutes to allow it to cool, then whisk vigorously until it can hold its shape.

Learning by Doing

If frosting doesn't hold its shape after 5 minutes of whisking, place in the refrigerator to allow it to cool completely.

5 Frost the muffins.

- When the muffins are completely cooled, use the offset frosting spreader to frost the muffins with the chocolate ganache frosting.

6 Dig in and enjoy!

Complete Your Meal

Dig in and enjoy with strawberries and a big glass of milk!

Practice Makes Perfect!

Beef Stir Fry

SERVES: 4

PREP TIME: 20 minutes 

READY TO EAT: 20 minutes 

Get Ready!

Ingredients

- 4 cups broccoli florets
- 1 lb boneless round steak
- 1 cup rice
- 1/3 cup soy sauce
- 1/3 cup water
- 1 small onion
- 3 T sesame oil
- 2 T brown sugar
- 1 T cornstarch
- 1 tsp ground ginger
- ½ tsp garlic powder

Utensils

- wok or large skillet
- saucepan
- clear measuring cup
- measuring cup set
- measuring spoon set
- whisk
- poly spoon

Get Set!

1. Cook the rice according to the package directions.
2. Slice steak into thin 3-inch strips.
3. In the clear measuring cup, whisk together the soy sauce, cornstarch, brown sugar, ginger, garlic powder, and 1/3 cup water.
4. Peel and chop the onion.

Get Cooking!

1. Heat 2 tablespoons of sesame oil over high heat in a wok or large skillet. When the pan is hot, add the beef and fry for 1–2 minutes or until it reaches desired doneness, or slightly less, stirring constantly. Remove to a plate and cover with foil to keep warm.
2. Add more oil to the pan if necessary, then add the broccoli florets and onion and stir-fry for 4–5 minutes or until slightly softened.
3. Return the beef to the pan along with the soy sauce mixture and cook another 1–2 minutes or until sauce thickens.
4. Dig in and enjoy over hot rice!

Raspberry Scones

SERVES: 8

PREP TIME: 20 minutes 

READY TO EAT: 45 minutes 

Get Ready!

Ingredients

- 2 cups flour
- 1 cup frozen raspberries
- ½ cup granulated sugar
- ½ cup heavy cream
- ½ cup butter (frozen)
- 1 egg
- 2 ½ tsp baking powder
- 1 tsp vanilla extract
- ½ tsp salt

Utensils

- mixing bowl set
- clear measuring cup
- measuring cup set
- measuring spoon set
- silicone mixing spatula
- cheese grater
- whisk
- cutting board

Get Set!

1. In the green mixing bowl, whisk together the flour, sugar, baking powder, and salt.
2. Grate the butter, then add to the flour. Use your fingers or a large fork to combine the butter and flour until it resembles coarse sand.
3. In the orange mixing bowl, whisk together the cream, egg, and vanilla. Add to the flour along with the frozen raspberries and toss the mixture with your silicone mixing spatula. (Dough will be a little wet.)
4. Work the dough into a ball with floured hands and form into an 8-inch disc. Cut the wedge into 8 triangles. Transfer the triangles to the baking tray.

Get Cooking!

1. Bake the scones for 20–25 minutes or until lightly golden and cooked through.
2. Remove from the oven and allow to cool for 5 minutes.
3. Dig in and enjoy warm with fresh fruit and yogurt!

Get Creative!

Zucchini Your Way

Zucchini is one of those vegetables that is good no matter how you cook it—or even if you don't! Plant some in a garden, and then enjoy them all summer long. The recipes below are just a sampling of all the ways to enjoy this versatile and delicious vegetable.

Baked Zucchini Chips

1. Slice 2 medium zucchini into ¼-inch slices.
2. Dip into 2 whisked eggs.
3. Coat with a mixture of ¼ cup breadcrumbs and ¼ cup Parmesan cheese.
4. Bake at 400°F for 10–15 minutes or until coating is golden brown and crisp.

Grilled Zucchini

1. Slice 2 medium zucchini lengthwise into ¼-inch wide slices.
2. Marinade in ½ cup Italian salad dressing for 15 minutes.
3. Grill until zucchini is tender.

Fresh Zucchini Salsa

1. Toss 2 chopped zucchini, ¼ cup cilantro, 1 chopped tomato, 1 chopped onion, 1 minced clove garlic and 1 cup corn with 1 tablespoon lime juice, 1 teaspoon salt, and a dash of cumin.
2. Refrigerate for about an hour and enjoy with tortilla chips.

Stuffed Zucchini Boats

1. Cut 2 large zucchini lengthwise and scoop out the insides.
2. Cook up the insides with ½ lb ground meat, 1 tomato, ½ an onion, 1 cup cooked rice, and 1–2 teaspoons of your favorite herbs and spices.
3. Fill the zucchini boats with the cooked mixture, top with grated cheese, and bake at 350°F for 15–20 minutes or until zucchini boats are fork tender.

Have Some Fun!

True or False?

Read each sentence below and decide whether the statement is true or false. If the sentence is true, circle the letter under the TRUE column. If the sentence is false, circle the letter under the FALSE column. When you're done, unscramble the circled letters in each column to find the missing phrase below.

	TRUE	FALSE
An apron is a good tool to use to pull a hot pan out of the oven.	p	f
White flour is healthier for you than whole-wheat flour.	r	i
A cheese grater can cut your fingers if you are not careful.	n	s
A whisk is a good tool to use to stir fry vegetables.	b	u
Milk can be turned into whipped cream.	l	m
A double boiler is a good tool to use to melt chocolate.	i	l
Zucchini needs to be peeled before you can eat them.	d	f
You should always check muffins for doneness before removing them from the oven.	t	c
Vanilla extract contains a lot of empty calories.	v	n

Unscramble the letters from the FALSE column in the lines below.

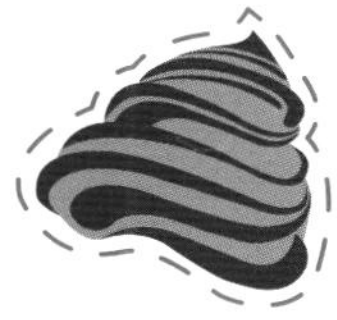

Unscramble the letters from the TRUE column in the lines below.

___ ___ ___

HINT: Something you need to make muffins.

Sausage and Potato Frittata

SERVES:
6–8

PREP TIME:
20 minutes

READY TO EAT:
30 minutes

Chefs-in-Training

What you'll learn:

- measuring skills
- grating cheese
- knife skills
- cracking eggs
- food safety

Shopping List

Got it!

- eggs (6)
- potato (1 small)
- onion (½)
- red bell pepper (½)
- breakfast sausage (¼ pound)
- cheddar cheese (4 ounces)
- fresh spinach (4 ounces)
- oil (2 T)
- salt (1 tsp)
- pepper (½ tsp)

Note to Grown Ups

There are lots of opportunities for your sous chef to practice knife skills in this recipe. The nylon plastic knives make it possible for kids to do all the chopping and dicing themselves with no worries of cutting little fingers. Pay attention though when they grate the cheese as the metal bumps on the grating plane are sharp.

What's On Your Plate?

Write the ingredients that are part of a healthy plate where they belong on the organizer.

potato

eggs

red bell pepper

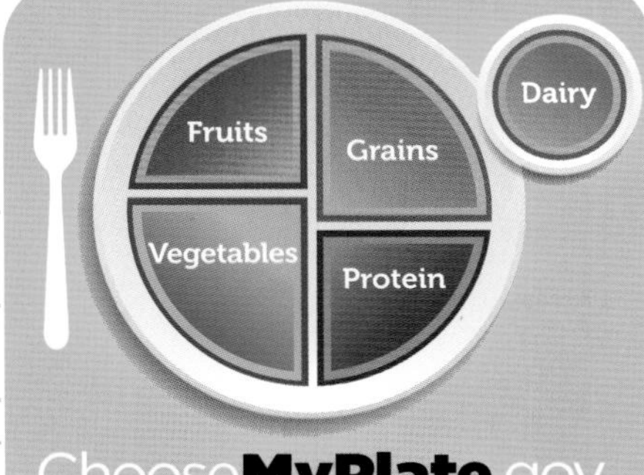

spinach

Cross out the ingredients that are not part of a healthy plate.

sausage

onion

cheese

spinach

Which two ingredients are a good source of iron?

Which four ingredients contain no fat?

CURIOUS CHEF FOOD FACTS

Dark green leafy vegetables like spinach and kale are a good source of iron, fiber and a whole bunch of essential vitamins and minerals. Be a healthier you and add greens to soups, eggs, stews, stir fries, spaghetti sauce, meatballs, even smoothies!

Get Ready!

Ingredients

eggs

potato

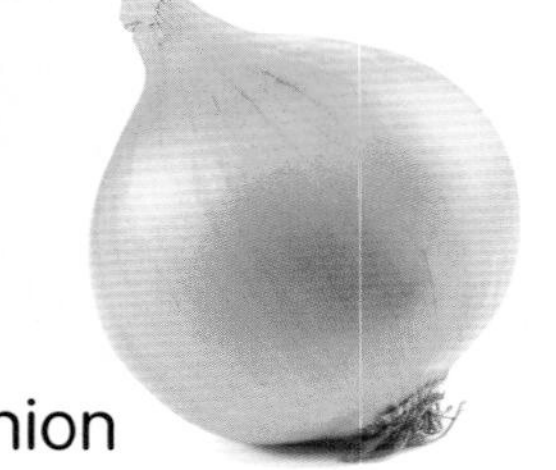

onion

red bell pepper

breakfast sausage

cheddar cheese

oil

fresh spinach

salt

pepper

Utensils

Cookware

- cast iron skillet
  (or other ovenproof skillet)

Measurement

- measuring spoon set

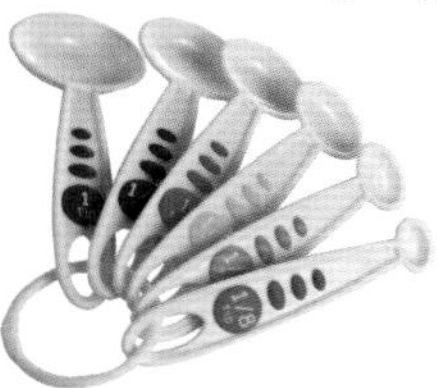

Tools

- vegetable scrubber
- cookie turner

- whisk
- nylon plastic knife
- nylon pie server
- cheese grater

Other

- 2 qt orange mixing bowl

- cutting board

Cultural Connection

Frittata is an egg-based dish enriched with vegetables and meats that originated in Italy. Use your research skills to find the country of origin of these common international dishes:

Food	Country of Origin
empanada	
piroshky	
spanakopita	
falafel	
latkas	
gyoza	

Get Set!

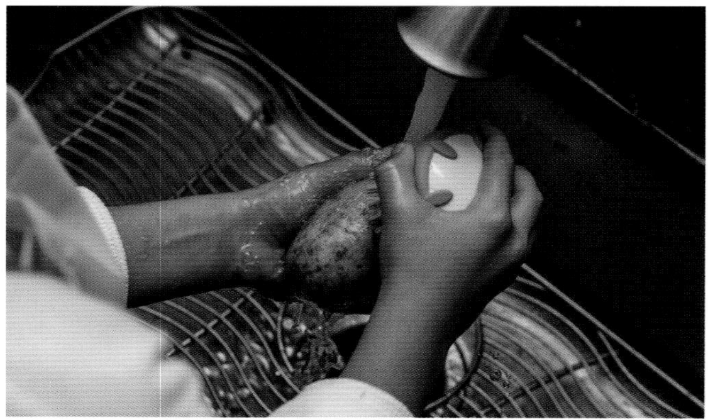

1 Precook the potato.

- Scrub the potato with the vegetable scrubber under cold running water.
- Poke the potato once with a fork to create holes for steam to escape.
- Cook in the microwave until you can easily poke a fork into it (about 5 minutes on high; time varies based on your microwave.)
- Allow to cool while completing the steps below.

2 Chop the onion and red pepper.

- Slice the red pepper in half lengthwise and remove the pith and seeds, then chop one half into ¼-inch pieces.
- Peel and chop half an onion into ¼-inch pieces.

3 Grate the cheese.

- Grate 1 cup of cheddar cheese.

Make sure you take pictures as you go through the steps!

Chop the spinach.

- Chop the spinach into small pieces using the nylon plastic knife.

5 Whisk the eggs.

- Crack the eggs into the orange mixing bowl.
- Whisk the eggs until they are thoroughly combined.

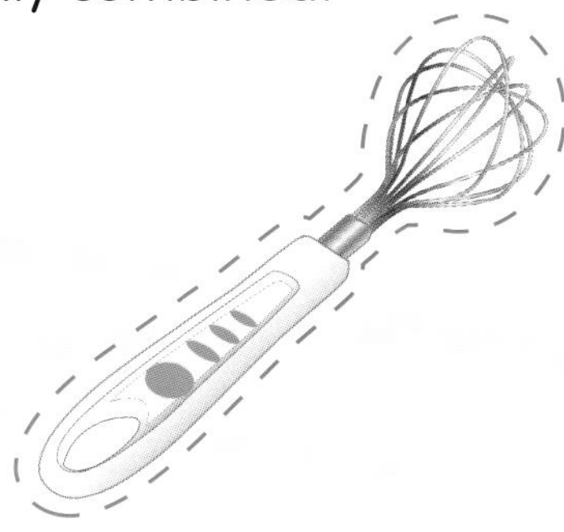

6 Dice the cooked potato.

- Chop the cooked potato into ½-inch pieces using your nylon plastic knife.

Get Cooking!

Cook the sausage.

- Remove the sausage from the casing.
- Place the sausage in the frying pan, then wash your hands in warm, soapy water.
- Cook the sausage over medium-high heat until it is no longer pink, breaking it up into small pieces with your cookie turner as it cooks.
- Transfer the cooked sausage to a paper towel and pat to absorb some of the grease.

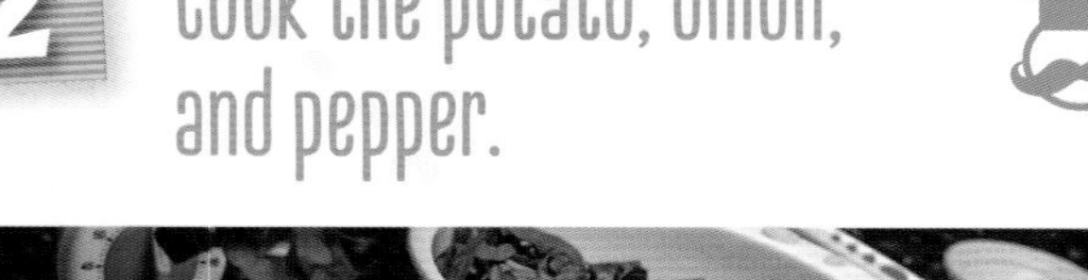

2 Cook the potato, onion, and pepper.

- Heat the oil in the hot skillet, then add the potatoes, onion, red bell pepper, 1 tsp salt, ½ tsp pepper.
- Cook over medium heat until the onions soften and turn clear and the potatoes are lightly browned.
- Reduce the heat to medium-low.

3 Cook the spinach.

- Add the chopped spinach to the skillet and cook until most of the liquid is cooked out of it.
- Return the sausage to the skillet.

Learning by Doing

Add spinach one handful at a time and let it cook down before adding more.

Make sure you take pictures as you go through the steps!

4 Add the eggs.

- Pour the eggs into the skillet and let them cook, undisturbed, for about 3 minutes or until the eggs are set on the edges but still loose on top.

Learning by Doing

Be careful not to let the eggs cook too long in the pan before placing them in the oven.

5 Bake the frittata.

- Sprinkle the cheese evenly over the eggs.
- Transfer the skillet to the oven and bake for 8–10 minutes or until the frittata is slightly golden and set in the middle.

6 Dig in and enjoy!

- Cut the frittata into wedges to serve.

Complete Your Meal

Dig in and enjoy with fresh fruit!

Practice Makes Perfect!

Banana Bread

SERVES: 2 loaves

PREP TIME: 15 minutes 

READY TO EAT: 1 hour 15 minutes 

Get Ready!

Ingredients

- 3 overripe bananas
- 2 cups flour
- 1 cup sugar
- ½ cup softened butter
- 2 eggs
- 3 T milk
- 1 T shortening
- 1 tsp vinegar
- 1 tsp baking soda
- ½ tsp vanilla extract

Utensils

- mixing bowl set
- pinch bowl
- measuring cup set
- measuring spoon set
- whisk
- potato masher
- poly spoon
- silicone mixing spatula
- 2 loaf pans
- wire cooling rack

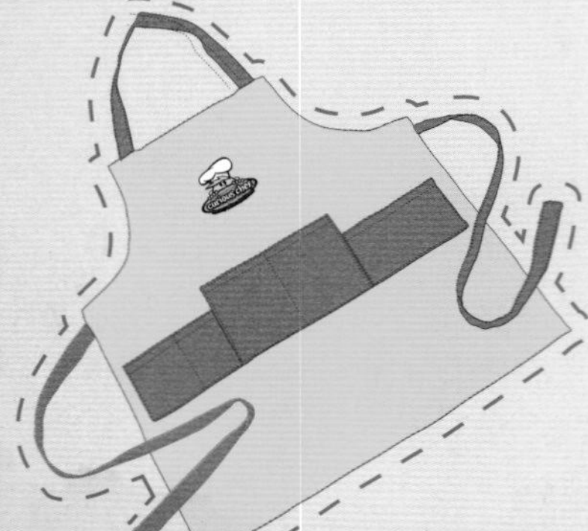

Get Set!

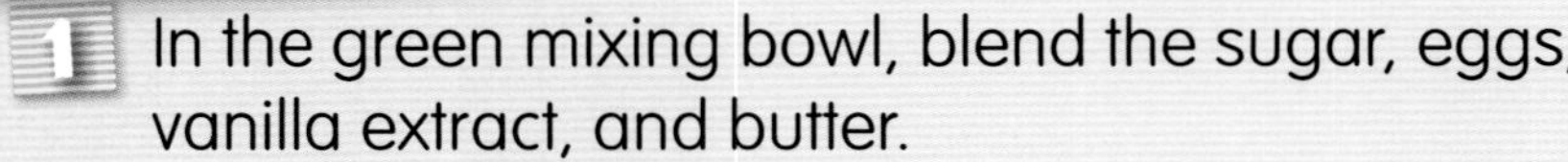

1. In the green mixing bowl, blend the sugar, eggs, vanilla extract, and butter.

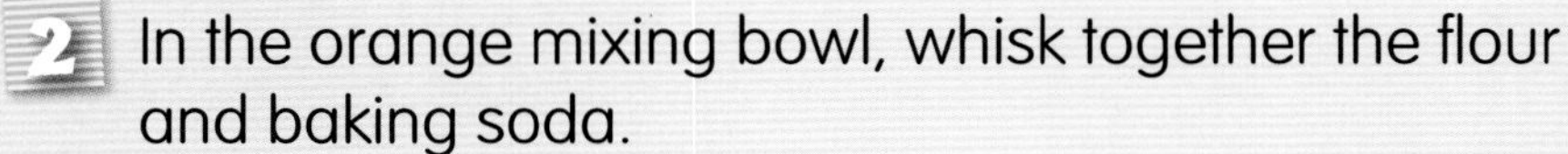

2. In the orange mixing bowl, whisk together the flour and baking soda.
3. In the pinch bowl, combine the milk and vinegar. Stir into the sugar mixture.
4. Gradually add the flour to the wet ingredients and stir to combine.
5. Add the bananas, smashing them as you stir them into the batter.
6. Grease the loaf pans with a thin layer of shortening. Add a teaspoon or so of flour and shake it around the pan to coat the inside of the pan. Shake out the extra flour.
7. Divide the batter equally between the two loaf pans.

Get Cooking!

1. Bake the loaves for 1 hour. Test for doneness by inserting a knife in the center.
2. Allow to cool in the pan for 5 minutes, then transfer to a wire cooling rack to cool completely.

Breakfast Crepes

SERVES: 8–10 crepes

PREP TIME: 30 minutes

READY TO EAT: 30 minutes

Get Ready!

Ingredients

- 2 cups flour
- 4 eggs
- 1 cup milk
- 1 cup water
- 8 oz softened cream cheese
- 1 jar jam or preserves
- ¼ cup vegetable oil
- 4 T butter, melted
- 4 tsp sugar
- 2 T maple syrup
- ½ tsp salt
- ½ tsp vanilla extract
- powdered sugar (for garnish)
- whipped cream (for garnish)

Utensils

- mixing bowl set
- whisk
- poly spoon
- clear measuring cup
- measuring spoon set
- measuring cup set
- silicone mixing spatula
- frying pan (small)

Get Set!

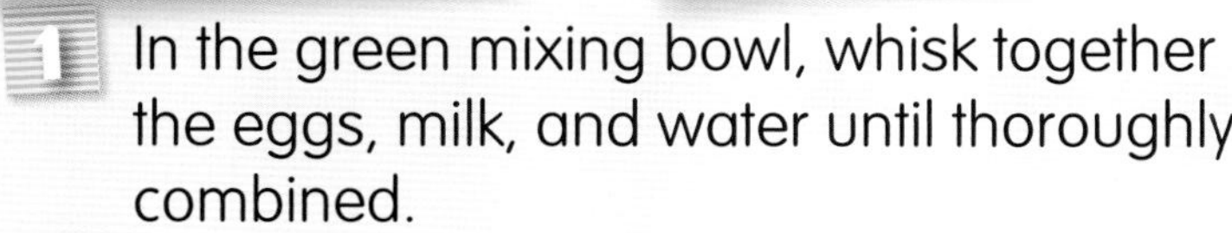

1. In the green mixing bowl, whisk together the eggs, milk, and water until thoroughly combined.
2. Gradually whisk in the flour until you have a smooth batter.
3. Whisk in the salt, sugar, and butter.
4. In the orange mixing bowl, combine the cream cheese, maple syrup and vanilla extract.

Get Cooking!

1. Heat the crepe pan over medium-high heat. Add just enough oil to coat the pan.
2. Pour about ¼ cup of batter into the pan and swirl the batter evenly around the pan.
3. Cook the crepe for about 1–2 minutes until the bottom is light brown.
4. Use the silicone mixing spatula to lift the crepe and turn it over. Cook another minute or until it is light brown.
5. Remove to a plate and cover with foil to keep warm.
6. Repeat steps 2–5 with the remaining batter.
7. Fill the crepes with the cream cheese mixture, then roll up.
8. Dig in and enjoy topped with jam or preserves or garnish with whipped cream and powdered sugar!

Get Creative!

Designer Frittata

Frittata is a great dish to know how to make because it's the kind of dish you can add pretty much anything you want to and it turns out great! Get your creative culinary juices flowing and create your own "designer frittata" made with all your favorite ingredients.

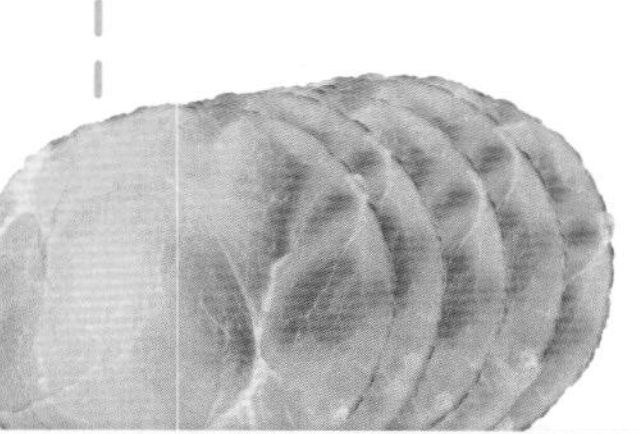

Have Some Fun!

Food Geography

The United States produces all kinds of food, and many of those foods are associated with certain states. Use the clues below to help you match the food with the state that is famous for it.

I can boast about having the southernmost point in the continental United States.

F

I am a the youngest state in America.

H

I am shaped like a chair.

I

I am known as the breadbasket of the country.

K

My name is also a girl's name.

G

I lie between the Mississippi and Missouri rivers.

I

I border two of the great lakes.

W

I border Mexico and the Pacific Ocean.

C

Chesapeake Bay forms my eastern border.

M

Some of my cities are below sea level.

L

My name is also what you call the hair on a horse's neck.

M

I am the largest state in America.

A

Ice Cream Sandwich Cookies

SERVES:
8 sandwiches

PREP TIME:
40 minutes

READY TO EAT:
1 hour 15 minutes

Chefs-in-Training

What you'll learn:

- measuring skills
- baking
- whisking
- separating eggs
- rolling out dough

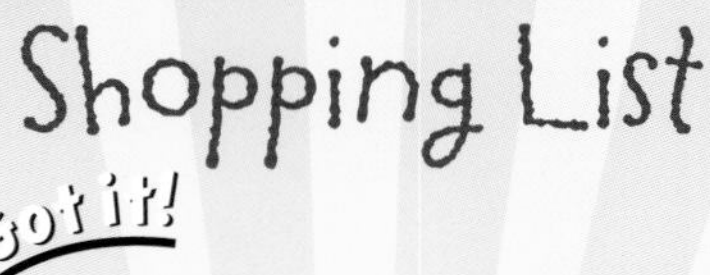

Shopping List

Got it!

- vanilla ice cream (1 qt)
- flour (2 cups)
- powdered sugar (1 ½ cups)
- butter (1 cup)
- eggs (2)
- cocoa powder (½ cup)
- sugar sprinkles (¼ cup)
- vanilla extract (1 tsp)
- salt (½ tsp)

Note to Grown Ups

Homemade ice cream sandwiches are a delicious and unique way for kids to "play" with their cookie cutters. Curious Chef cookie cutters, with their oversized shape and soft-touch grip, let kids be successful and safe while they are baking up some fun!

What's On Your Plate?

Write the ingredients that are part of a healthy plate where they belong on the organizer.

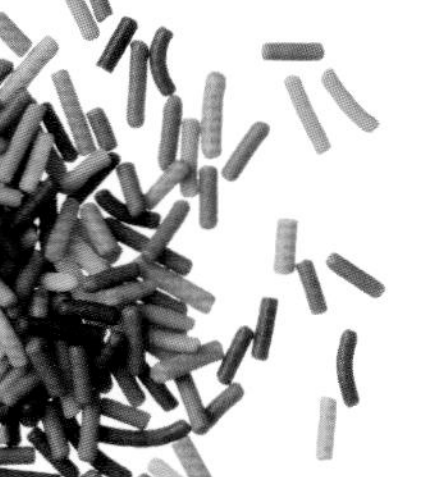

sugar sprinkles

eggs

ice cream

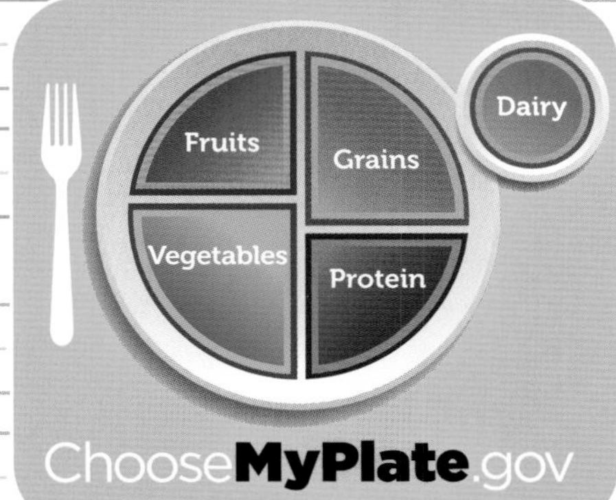

Cross out the ingredients that are not part of a healthy plate.

ice cream

powdered sugar

flour

butter

Which ingredient is a solid fat high in empty calories?

How many ingredients in this recipe are considered healthy?

CURIOUS CHEF FOOD FACTS

Ice cream is made mostly from milk and cream, which is the fat in milk. Not everyone can eat dairy products though, so there are also non-dairy versions available that are made with ingredients like coconut milk, almond milk, and soy milk.

Get Ready!

Ingredients

flour

cocoa powder

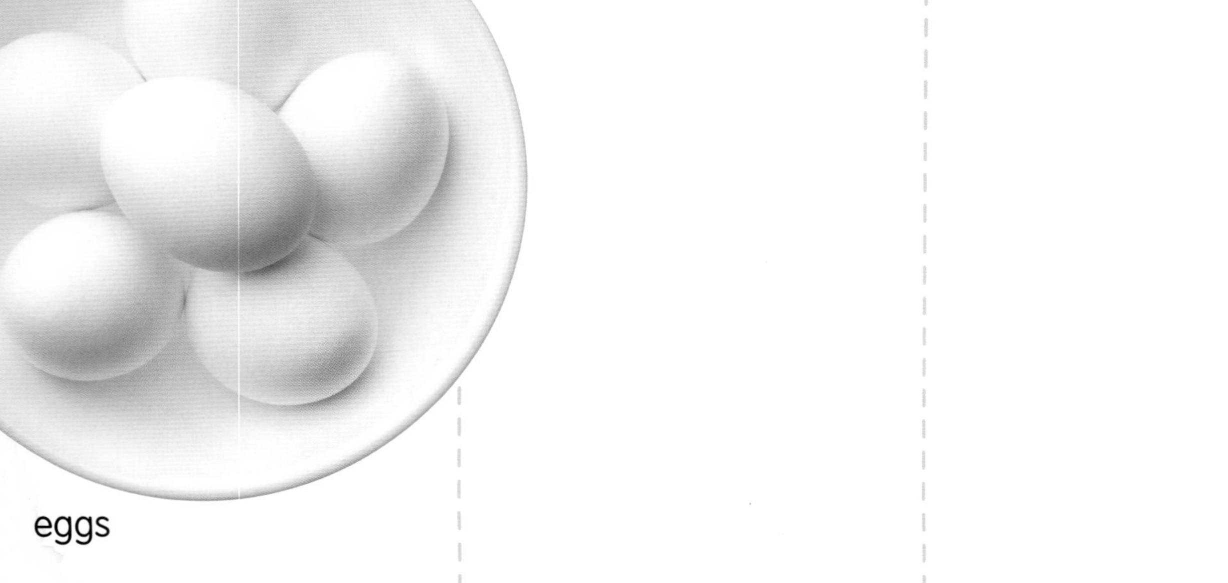

eggs

powdered sugar

butter

vanilla extract

salt

sugar sprinkles

ice cream

Utensils

Cookware

- cookie sheet

- 9-x-13 inch baking dish

Measurement

- measuring cup set

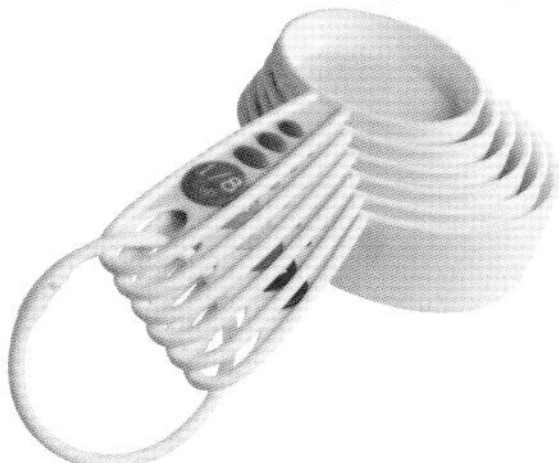

- measuring spoon set

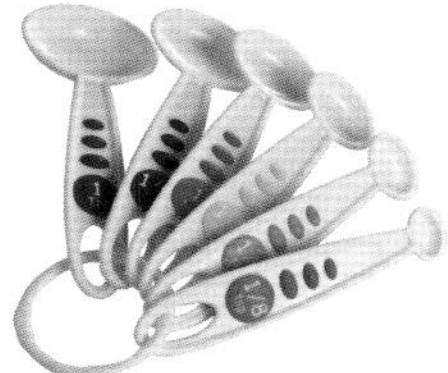

Tools

- poly spoon
- cookie turner
- rolling pin
- whisk
- offset frosting spreader

- cookie cutter collection

Other

- 3 qt green mixing bowl

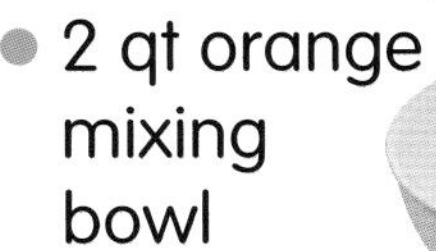

- 2 qt orange mixing bowl
- pinch bowl

- prep bowl set

- wire cooling rack
- plastic wrap
- parchment or wax paper

Art Connection

Get creative with your cookie cutter collection and create a work of art. Trace cookie cutters on paper and then color them in with crayons or glue and glitter. Let your imagination guide you as you create your cookie cutter masterpiece!

Get Set!

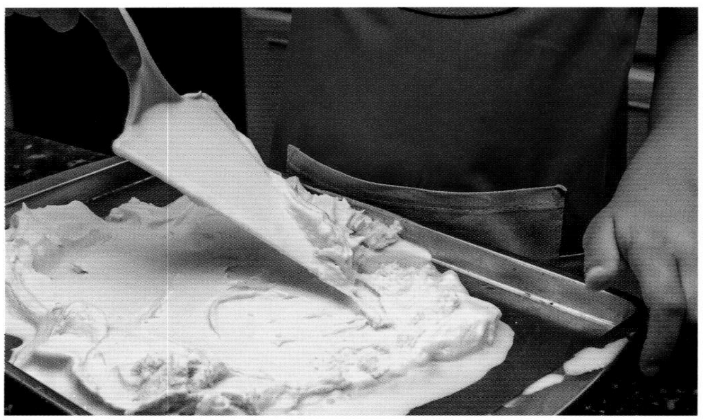

- Take out the ice cream and allow it to soften for about 20 minutes while completing the other steps.
- When the ice cream is soft, use the nylon pie server to spread it evenly into a 9-x-13 baking pan lined with plastic wrap.
- Cover with plastic wrap and return to freezer.

1 Prepare the ice cream.

- In the orange mixing bowl, measure:
  - 2 cups flour
  - ½ cup cocoa powder
  - ½ tsp salt
- Use your whisk to combine the ingredients.

2 Measure the dry ingredients.

- In the green mixing bowl, measure and combine:
  - 1 cup (2 sticks) softened butter
  - 1 ½ cups powdered sugar
  - 2 egg yolks
  - 1 tsp vanilla extract
- Blend ingredients with the poly spoon until smooth.

3 Blend the wet ingredients.

Make sure you take pictures as you go through the steps!

4 Finish the cookie dough.

- Stir the flour into the butter mixture a little bit at a time.
- Mix until a firm dough forms.
- Shape the dough into two discs.
- Wrap in plastic and chill for 20 minutes.

5 Roll out the cookies.

- Roll the chilled dough into a ¼-inch thick sheet.

Learning by Doing

Dust the dough with flour as often as needed to keep it from sticking.

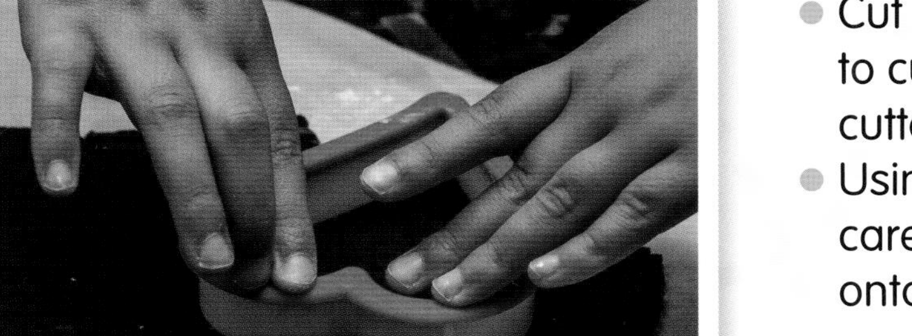

6 Cut out the cookies.

- Cut out cookies, being sure to cut out 2 cookies for each cutter used.
- Using your cookie turner, carefully transfer the cookies onto a cookie sheet lined with parchment paper.
- Poke each cookie 4 to 6 times with a fork.

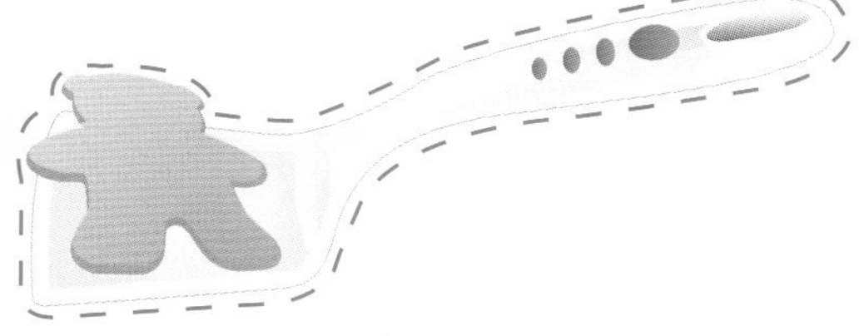

Get Cooking!

1 Bake the cookies.

- Bake the cookies for 8–10 minutes, checking frequently to make sure they don't get overcooked.
- Remove to a wire rack to cool completely before assembling the sandwiches.

2 Cut out the ice cream.

- Remove the ice cream from the baking pan and place on a solid surface.
- Cut ice cream into shapes to match the cookies (1 ice cream cut out for 2 cookie cut outs.)

Learning by Doing

Dip the cookie cutters in warm water to make it easier to cut through the ice cream.

A Healthier You

Ice cream, as the name implies, is made with cream, so it is high in fat calories. Frozen yogurt is not made from cream so it offers a delicious and lower-fat alternative to ice cream. Be a healthier you and choose frozen yogurt next time you're craving a sweet, creamy, frozen treat!

Make sure you take pictures as you go through the steps!

3 Assemble the sandwiches.

- Place an ice cream cut out between two cookies of a matching shape.
- Hold the sandwiches over a bowl and sprinkle the sugar sprinkles to cover the ice cream edge.

4 Dig in and enjoy!

- Dig in and enjoy your sandwich with sliced bananas or other fresh fruit!

Complete Your Meal

Dig in and enjoy with fresh fruit!

Practice Makes Perfect!

Raspberry Bark

SERVES:	PREP TIME:	READY TO EAT:
8	15 minutes	2 hour 15 minutes

Get Ready!

Ingredients

- 16 oz dark chocolate (sweetened or semi-sweet)
- ½ lb raspberries
- 1 T shortening
- powdered sugar (for garnish)

Utensils

- double boiler, or a large saucepan and a glass or metal bowl that fits inside the saucepan without touching the bottom
- baking tray
- poly spoon
- cookie cutter collection
- colander

Get Set!

1. Rinse the raspberries in the colander under cold running water. Gently pat dry with a paper towel.
2. Rub shortening on the inside of 8 cookie cutters. Arrange them on a baking tray lined with parchment paper.
3. Fill the saucepan with just enough water so that the bottom of the bowl, when inserted, does not touch the water.
4. Break the chocolate into small pieces.

Get Cooking!

1. Place the chocolate pieces in the bowl. Melt the chocolate over medium-low heat, stirring frequently.
2. Fill the cookie cutters about half full of chocolate.
3. Place raspberries upside down into the chocolate to fill the cookie cutters.
4. Refrigerate for about an hour or until chocolate is firm. Carefully remove the cookie cutters from the chocolate.
5. Reheat the remaining chocolate and drizzle it in thin stripes over the raspberries.
6. Chill another 30-60 minutes, garnish with powdered sugar, then dig in and enjoy!

Fruit Tart Hearts

SERVES: 8

PREP TIME: 10 minutes

READY TO EAT: 1 hour 10 minutes

Get Ready!

Ingredients

- 2 ¼ cups flour
- 1 cup butter, cold and diced into small cubes
- 1 cup powdered sugar
- ¾ cup strawberry preserves
- 4–6 T ice water
- 2 T (or more) half-and-half
- 1 tsp salt
- 1 tsp sugar
- ¼ tsp vanilla extract
- colored sprinkles

Utensils

- mixing bowl set
- poly spoon
- whisk
- heart cookie cutter
- measuring spoon set
- measuring cup set
- offset frosting spreader
- plastic wrap

Get Set!

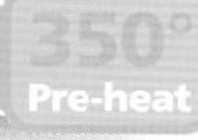

1. Combine the flour, salt, sugar and butter until it looks like coarse sand. Add ice water a few tablespoons at a time until dough is no longer sticky. Wrap in plastic and chill 1 hour.
2. Roll chilled dough into 2 sheets about ¼ inch thick. Cut out an even number of heart shapes. Place half the hearts on a baking tray lined with parchment paper. Place about 2 tablespoons of preserves in the center of each heart.
3. Top each with another heart. Seal the seams tightly with your fingers, then reseal using the tines of a fork.

Get Cooking!

1. Bake at 350°F for 25–30 minutes or until they turn golden brown.
2. While the tarts are baking, whisk the powdered sugar, cream and vanilla extract together until smooth. Add more cream as necessary to reach the desired consistency.
3. When tarts are completely cooled, use the offset frosting spreader to frost the tarts and top with colored sprinkles.

Get Creative!

Homemade Playdough

You're cooking skills come in handy for more than just making something to eat. Put your new skills to work making playdough. Then have some fun cutting out shapes with your cookie cutter collection!

What You'll Need:

- 2 cups flour
- 2 tablespoons vegetable oil
- ½ cup of salt
- 2 tablespoons cream of tartar
- 1 ½ cup boiling water
- gel food dye (in variety of colors)
- 3 quart green mixing bowl
- measuring spoon set
- measuring cup set
- clear measuring cup
- poly spoon
- rolling pin
- cookie cutters
- rubber gloves (optional)

What You'll Do:

1. In the green mixing bowl, whisk together the flour, salt and cream of tartar.
2. Add 2 tablespoons of oil and stir with your poly spoon to combine.
3. Pour in the boiling water.
4. Mix all the ingredients together until they form the dough.
5. After it's cooled, separate the dough into balls, one for each different color you want to make.
6. Make an indentation in the dough ball so you have a little bowl to pour the gel food dye in to.
7. Drip your gel dye into the bowls, or mix dye colors if you want to make another color.
8. Put on gloves to keep your hands clean, then knead the dough until the dye is thoroughly mixed.
9. Roll out the dough with your rolling pin, then have some fun cutting out shapes with your cookie cutters.

Have Some Fun!

Kitchen Scavenger Hunt

Your kitchen is full of all kinds of things—cooking utensils, food, cleaning supplies, and appliances, large and small. Go on a kitchen scavenger hunt and have some fun exploring all the things in your kitchen. For a real challenge, set a time limit and see who can find the most items. Happy hunting!

A food item made from whole-grains.

A fruit or vegetable that has a lot of vitamin C in it.

A tool for measuring liquids.

A tool for handling hot things.

An electrical appliance, other than your stove, which is used to cook food.

Something you use to wash the dishes.

A tool for removing the peel from an apple.

A tool for turning cream into whipped cream.

Something that is used to store food and keep it fresh.

A tool you can use to flip a pancake.

Something you should never use without adult supervision.

A food item that contains a lot of empty calories.

A food item that contains a lot of sugar.

A food item that is a good source of calcium.

Baked Peaches 'n Cream

SERVES:
4–8

PREP TIME:
35 minutes

READY TO EAT:
35 minutes

Chefs-in-Training

What you'll learn:

- measuring skills
- mixing skills
- toasting nuts
- food safety
- pitting peaches

Shopping List

Got it!

- ○ peaches (4)
- ○ mascarpone (1 cup)
- ○ heavy whipping cream (½ cup)
- ○ sliced almonds (4 oz)
- ○ butter (¼ cup)
- ○ honey (¼ cup)
- ○ sugar (2 T)
- ○ cinnamon (1 tsp)
- ○ vanilla extract (1 tsp)

Note to Grown Ups

This recipe is very simple to prepare for even the youngest sous chefs. The serving tongs with their soft-touch button grips are the perfect tool for handling the hot, baked peaches. But your sous chef's favorite step will probably be when they get to use the pastry brush to "paint" the peaches with butter.

What's On Your Plate?

Write the ingredients that are part of a healthy plate where they belong on the organizer.

almonds

honey

butter

peaches

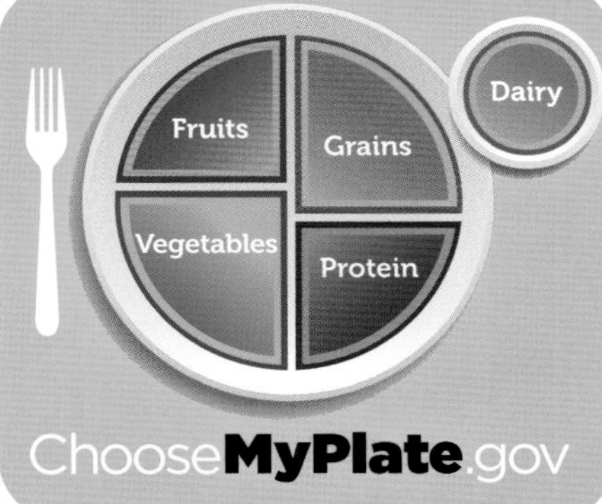

Cross out the ingredients that are not part of a healthy plate.

cream

peaches

sugar

Which ingredient contains the healthiest kind of fat?

Which ingredients are a less healthy source of fat?

CURIOUS CHEF FOOD FACTS

When buying peaches, select firm, unbruised peaches with nice color. To ripen, cover them with a linen napkin, cotton cloth, or pillowcase. Keep them in a cool place out of the sun and wait patiently. When they smell like peaches, they are ripe, which could take up to 5 days.

Get Ready!

Ingredients

peaches

butter

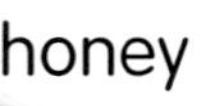

honey

mascarpone

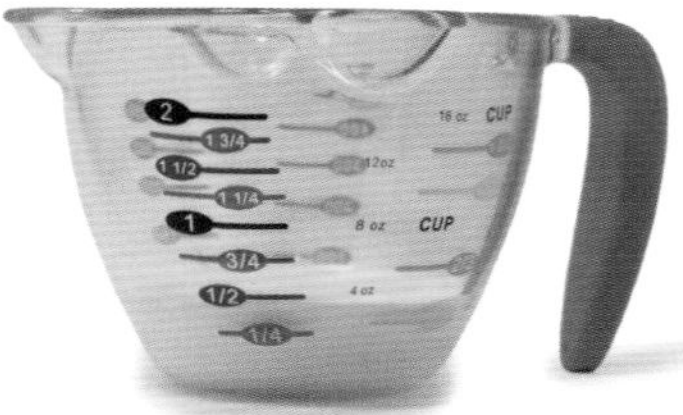

whipping cream

vanilla extract

sliced almonds

sugar

cinnamon

Utensils

Cookware

- baking dish

- frying pan (large)

Measurement

- measuring spoon set

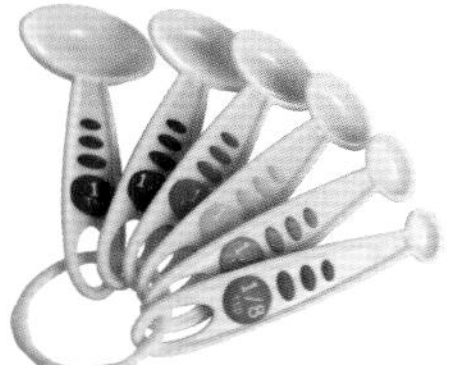

- measuring cup set

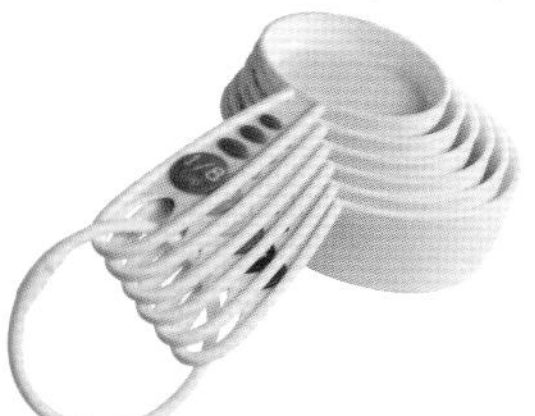

- clear measuring cup

Tools

- poly spoon
- nylon plastic knife
- pastry brush
- serving tongs
- silicone mixing spatula

Other

- 2 qt orange mixing bowl

- 1 qt yellow mixing bowl

- prep bowl set

- pinch bowl set
- cutting board

Science Connection

Watch science in action by growing your own peach tree from the pits. Here's how:

1. **Clean off any fruit that is stuck in the grooves of the pits.**
2. **Soak them in water for 30 minutes, then set it on a damp paper towel and seal in a plastic zipper bag.**
3. **Place the pits in the refrigerator for six weeks, then plant the sprouted pits outside in a sunny location.**

NOTE: Sprouted seeds need to be planted in the fall.

Get Set!

- Wash the peaches under cold running water.
- Pat dry with a paper towel.

 Wash the peaches. 

- Slice the peaches in half with your nylon plastic knife along the natural crease in the peach.

2 Slice the peaches.

- Use your nylon plastic knife to remove the peach pits.

3 Pit the peaches.

Make sure you take pictures as you go through the steps!

- Place the butter in the yellow mixing bowl and melt in the microwave.
- Use your pastry brush to apply a generous amount of melted butter to each peach half.
- Drizzle each peach half with a generous amount of honey.

4 Prepare to bake the peaches.

- In a pinch bowl, combine 2 tablespoons sugar and 1 teaspoon cinnamon.
- Stir to thoroughly combine the sugar and cinnamon.

5 Prepare the cinnamon sugar.

A Healthier You

Fruit is not only good eaten fresh as a snack, it also makes delicious desserts that are good for you. Be a healthier you and look for dessert recipes that are made with more fruit and less white flour, butter, and sugar.

Get Cooking!

1 Bake the peaches.

- Bake the peaches for 25–30 minutes. Keep an eye on them to make sure they brown but don't burn.

Learning by Doing

Set your timer for 20 minutes and check the peaches to make sure they aren't getting overcooked.

2 Make the cream topping.

- Into the orange mixing bowl, measure the mascarpone, whipping cream, and vanilla extract.
- Use your poly spoon to stir the ingredients until they are thoroughly combined and the mixture is smooth and creamy.

3 Toast the almonds.

- Heat the frying pan over medium heat.
- Add the sliced almonds and toast the almonds for 1–2 minutes until they just begin to brown, stirring often.

Learning by Doing

Nuts burn quickly so it is important to remove them from the pan as soon as they start to brown.

Make sure you take pictures as you go through the steps!

4 Add the cream topping.

- Remove the baked peaches to a serving plate using your serving tongs.
- Spoon any juices from the baking dish over the peaches.
- Top each peach with a heaping spoonful of the mascarpone cream.
- Sprinkle the toasted almonds evenly over the peaches.

5 Dig in and enjoy!

- Dig in and enjoy topped with a light sprinkling of the cinnamon sugar.

Complete Your Meal

Dig in and enjoy with a glass of milk!

Practice Makes Perfect!

Chocolate Custard Tarts

SERVES: 6

PREP TIME: 30 minutes  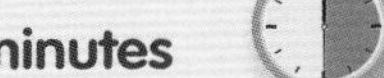

READY TO EAT: 1 hour 

Get Ready!

Ingredients

- 1 ½ cups heavy cream
- 1 can whipped cream
- 1 can refrigerated pie crust
- 3 eggs
- ¼ cup sugar
- 3 oz dark chocolate
- 1 tsp vanilla extract
- ¼ tsp salt

Utensils

- double boiler
- measuring cup set
- measuring spoon set
- 1 qt yellow mixing bowl
- clear measuring cup
- muffin tin
- rolling pin
- flower cookie cutter
- silicone mixing spoon
- nylon plastic knife

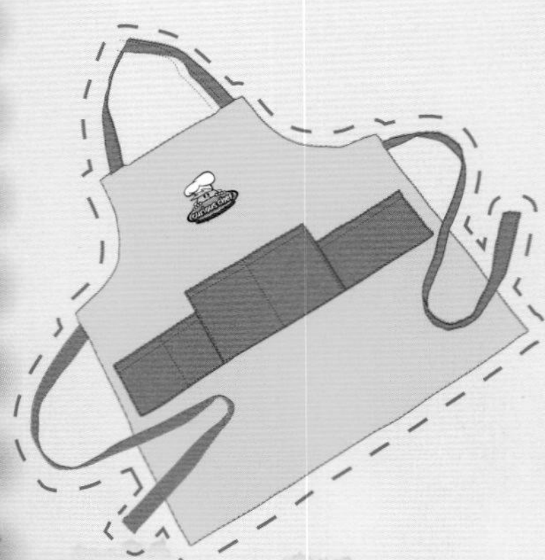

Get Set!

1. Roll out the pie crust and cut out six flowers. Line each muffin cup with a flower cut out. Poke the bottom of each pastry shell twice with a fork.
2. Separate 3 egg yolks into the yellow mixing bowl.
3. Coarsely chop the chocolate.

Get Cooking!

1. Bake the shells for 5–7 minutes or until lightly browned around the edges.
2. Heat the heavy cream, vanilla extract, sugar, and salt in the double boiler over medium-high heat. Whisk until the cream is hot and the sugar is dissolved.
3. Spoon a bit of the hot cream into the egg yolks and whisk to combine. Pour the egg mixture back into the double boiler and add the chocolate. Cook for 2–3 minutes, stirring continuously. Cook until it is thick enough to coat the back of a spoon.
4. Spoon the custard into the baked pie shells. Refrigerate for about 30 minutes.
5. Dig in and enjoy the chilled tarts with a dollop of whipped cream or fresh fruit!

Parmesan Cheddar Crackers

SERVES: 18 crackers

PREP TIME: 30 minutes 

READY TO EAT: 30 minutes 

Get Ready!

Ingredients

- 2 ½ cups grated cheddar cheese
- 1 ½ cups flour
- 1 ½ cups grated Parmesan cheese
- ½ cup butter, softened
- 5 T half-and-half
- 3 T dried basil
- 1 tsp salt

Utensils

- 3 qt green mixing bowl
- baking tray
- measuring spoon set
- measuring cup set
- poly spoon
- rolling pin
- cookie cutter (or round cup)
- cookie turner
- wire cooling rack
- parchment paper

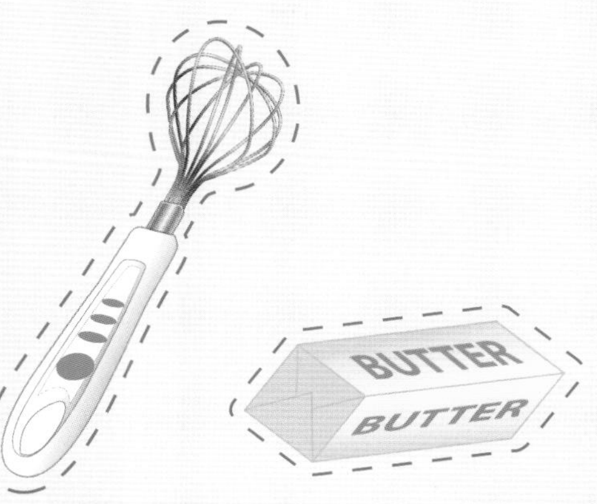

Get Set!

1. Use your poly spoon to combine the cheddar cheese, butter, half-and-half, and salt.
2. Gradually add the flour, Parmesan cheese, and basil. Stir just until the ingredients are combined, adding more cream as necessary.
3. Roll out the dough onto a well-floured surface, then divide into 3 equal portions.
4. Roll each portion out into an even 1/8-inch thick sheet.
5. Dip your cutter in flour and cut out a cracker. Repeat for each cracker you cut out.
6. Place cut outs 1-inch apart on parchment paper-lined baking trays.

Get Cooking!

1. Bake the crackers for 10 minutes, then flip over and bake another 5 minutes or until they turn golden brown.
2. Use your cookie turner to remove the crackers to a wire rack to cool.
3. Dig in and enjoy with your favorite cracker dip!

Get Creative!

Peachy Possibilities

Getting creative with peaches is easy. Whether you enjoy them baked, fresh, frozen, or blended, you'll always end up with a healthy and delicious treat. Check out the possibilities below and then see what other fresh ideas they might spark for you!

Fresh Peach Salsa

What You'll Need:

- 1 lb tomatoes, diced
- 1 bell pepper, seeded and finely diced
- 2 mild chili peppers, seeded and finely diced
- 1 medium onion, finely diced
- 1 ½ lbs peaches, diced
- ½ bunch cilantro, chopped
- 2 T lime juice
- 1 ½ tsp salt
- ¼ tsp pepper

What You'll Do:

1. Place everything in a big bowl and stir gently to combine.
2. Cover with plastic wrap and refrigerate for 30 minutes to allow the flavors to mingle.
3. Serve with tortilla chips or crackers.

Blended Peach Smoothie

What You'll Need:

- 1–2 peaches, cut into chunks
- ½ cup vanilla yogurt
- ½ cup milk
- ¼ teaspoon vanilla extract
- 1 cup ice cubes or ½ cup crushed ice

What You'll Do:

1. Blend everything in a blender until smooth, adding more milk as needed to reach desired thickness.
2. Serve immediately.

Frozen Peach Yogurt

What You'll Need:

- 4 cups fresh peaches (cut up and frozen solid)
- 3 tablespoons honey
- ½ cup plain yogurt
- 1 tablespoon fresh lemon juice

What You'll Do:

1. Place everything in a blender or food processor and blend until smooth and creamy.
2. Serve immediately or store in the freezer.

Have Some Fun!

Which One Is Different?

In each row there is one item that starts with a different letter than all the rest. Circle those items and write the letter each one starts with on the blank line at the beginning of the row. Then, unscramble the letters to find the answer to the question below.

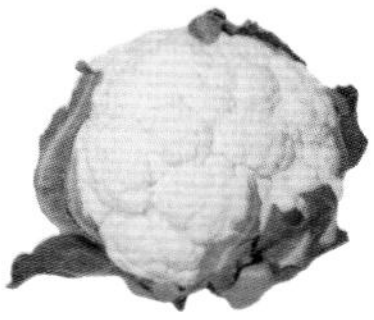

Which fruit has only one seed inside?

Quiche Lorraine

SERVES:
6–8

PREP TIME:
30 minutes

READY TO EAT:
1 hour 30 minutes

Chefs-in-Training

What you'll learn:
- making pie crust
- whisking
- measuring skills
- frying bacon
- chopping onions

Shopping List

Got it!

- ○ bacon (8 slices)
- ○ eggs (4 large)
- ○ cream (2 cups)
- ○ flour (1 ½ cups)
- ○ onion (1 medium)
- ○ Swiss or Gruyere cheese (½ lb)
- ○ shortening (⅓ cup)
- ○ salt (½ tsp)

Note to Grown Ups

This is a great learning recipe because kids get to practice with so many different skills and tools. Having the caddy with all their tools handy in one place keeps kids organized and the work area neat and tidy. Kids can complete all the Get Set! steps on their own except for slicing the bacon. This requires a sharp metal knife so they will need your help with this step.

Caddy Collection

What's On Your Plate?

Write the ingredients that are part of a healthy plate where they belong on the organizer.

eggs

milk

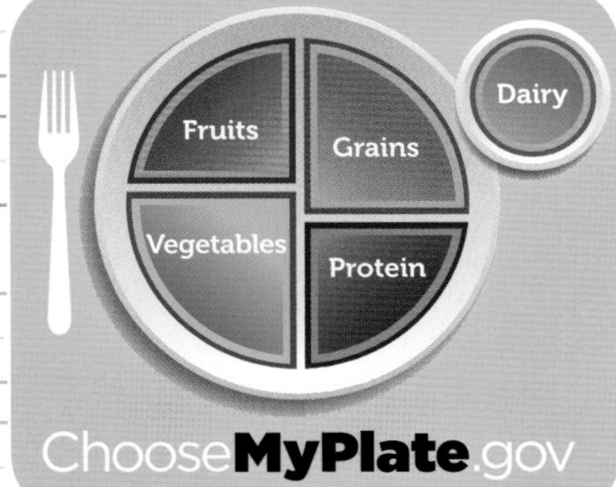

bacon

cheese

Cross out the ingredients that are not part of a healthy plate.

onion

bacon

flour

Which ingredient belongs in two categories on the healthy plate organizer?

Which four ingredients come from animals?

CURIOUS CHEF FOOD FACTS

Eggs are a delicious way to give yourself a health boost. They have a very high quality protein and are full of all sorts of other essential nutrients like calcium and iron. They also have lots of vitamins, including vitamins A and B2, which help your body grow.

Get Ready!

Ingredients

flour

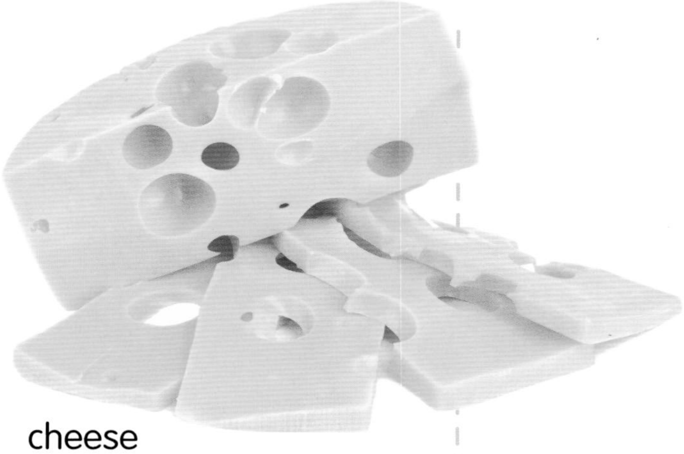

cheese

shortening

bacon

onion

eggs

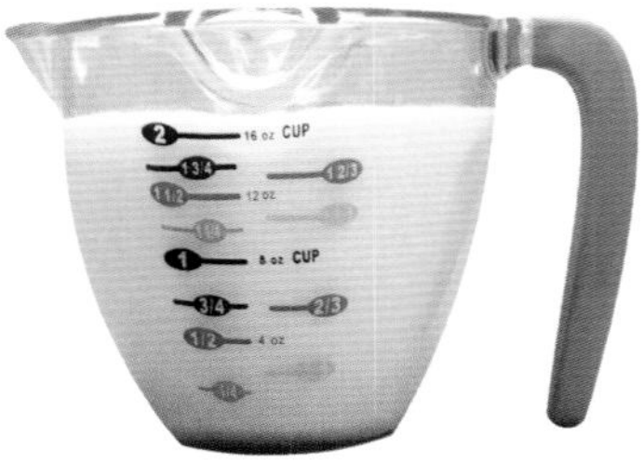

cream

salt

Utensils

Cookware

- metal pie tin

- frying pan (large)

Measurement

- measuring cup set

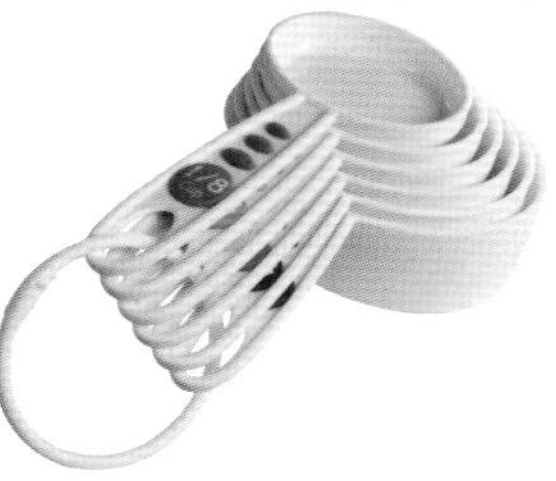

- measuring spoon set

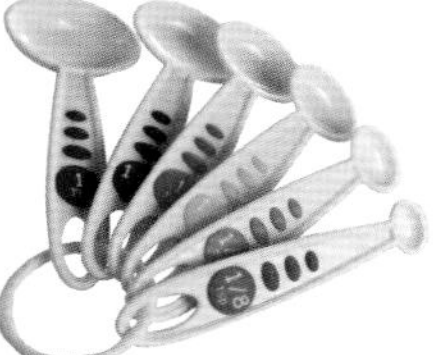

- clear measuring cup

Tools

- poly spoon

- whisk

- nylon plastic knife
- rolling pin

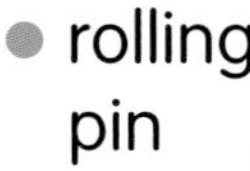

- cookie turner

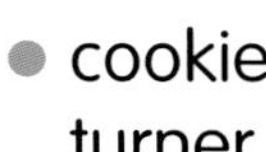

- nylon pie server
- cheese grater

Other

- 3 qt green mixing bowl
- 2 qt orange mixing bowl

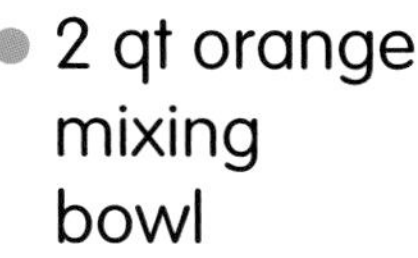

- prep bowl set

- cutting board

- plastic wrap

Cultural Connection

Although we think of quiche as a French dish, the word "quiche" actually comes from the German word "kuchen," which means cake. Quiche was originally made in the medieval German kingdom of Lothringen, but the French later changed the name to Lorraine. Today, quiche Lorraine is one of the most popular kinds of quiche.

Get Set!

Make the pie dough.

- Into the green mixing bowl, measure:
  - 1 ½ cups flour
  - ⅓ cup shortening
  - 1 tsp salt
- Mix together with your poly spoon until it looks like coarse sand.
- Add 5–6 tablespoons of water, 1–2 at a time, until the dough sticks together in a ball.
- Form into a disc and wrap in plastic wrap.
- Chill in the refrigerator for 15 minutes.

Roll out the pie crust.

- Using your rolling pin, roll the dough out on a floured surface to form a 13-inch circle.

- Gently lift the dough and place it in the pie tin.
- Pinch the extra dough around the edges to form a thick outer rim.

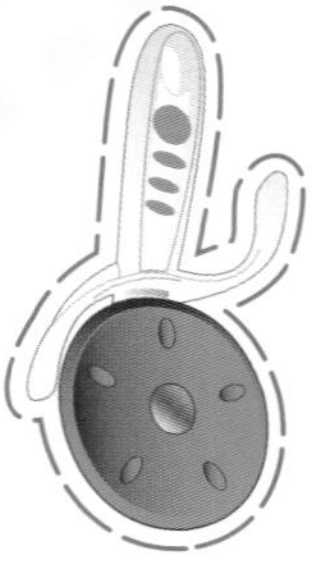

Make sure you take pictures as you go through the steps!

3 Grate the cheese.

- Grate the Swiss or Gruyere cheese.

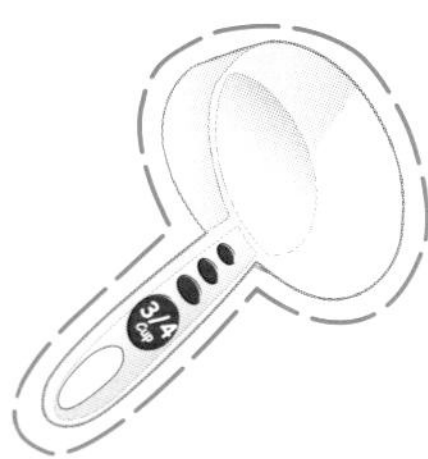

4 Make the filling.

- Into the orange mixing bowl, whisk together:
  - 4 eggs
  - 2 cups cream
  - 1 tsp salt

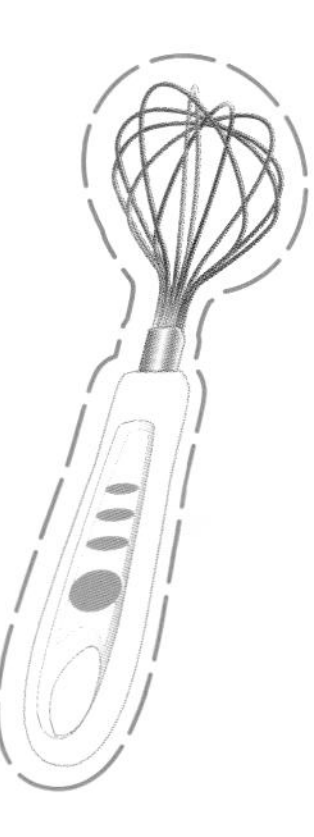

5 Chop the onion and bacon.

- Chop the onion into ¼-inch pieces.
- Using a sharp, metal knife, slice the bacon into 1-inch pieces.
- Wash your hands with warm, soapy water.

Get Cooking!

- Cook the bacon in the large frying pan over medium-high heat until it's brown and crispy.
- Remove bacon pieces to a paper towel.
- Drain the grease from the pan and return it to the stove.

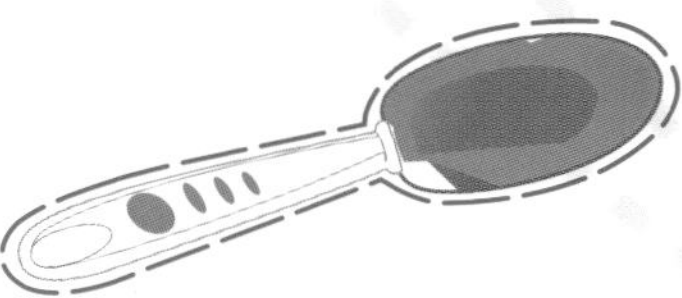

1 Fry the bacon.

- Cook the onions in the large frying pan until they soften and turn clear.

2 Cook the onions.

- Fill the pie crust with the bacon, onions and cheese.
- Pour the custard mixture into the pie to within a half inch from the top of the crust.

3 Assemble the quiche.

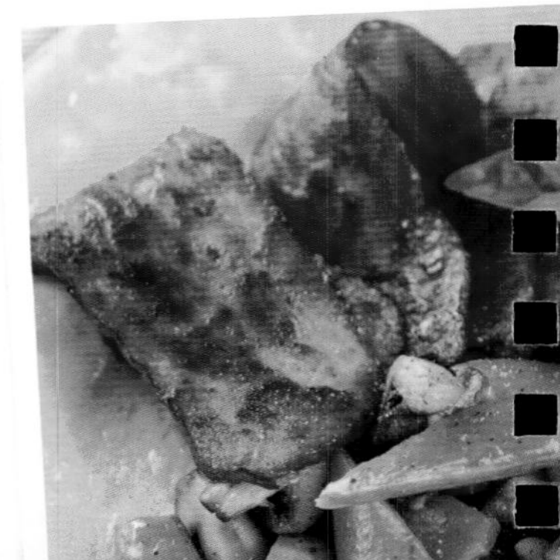

Make sure you take pictures as you go through the steps!

Bake the quiche.

- Bake the quiche, uncovered, for 45 minutes or until a knife inserted in the center comes out clean.

Dig in and enjoy!

- Allow the quiche to cool for 15–20 minutes.
- Use your nylon pie server to dish up individual servings.

healthy food!

A Healthier You

Bacon is a good source of protein but it is also very high in saturated fat (almost three quarters of the calories in bacon come from fat!) Limit how much bacon you eat or choose leaner varieties made from turkey or soy.

Complete Your Meal

Dig in and enjoy with fresh fruit or hash browns!

Practice Makes Perfect!

Fruit Salsa and Chips

SERVES: 4–6

PREP TIME: 20 minutes 

READY TO EAT: 45 minutes 

Get Ready!

Ingredients

- 16 oz strawberries, diced
- 8 oz raspberries
- 2 kiwis, peeled and diced
- 2 apples, peeled, cored and diced
- ¼ cup sugar
- 3 T fruit preserves
- 1 T brown sugar
- 10 flour tortillas
- 2 T sugar
- 2 T cinnamon
- 1 T butter, melted

Utensils

- baking tray
- 3 qt green mixing bowl
- pinch bowl set
- nylon plastic knife
- fruit & vegetable peeler
- apple slicer
- pastry brush
- nylon pizza cutter
- cutting board

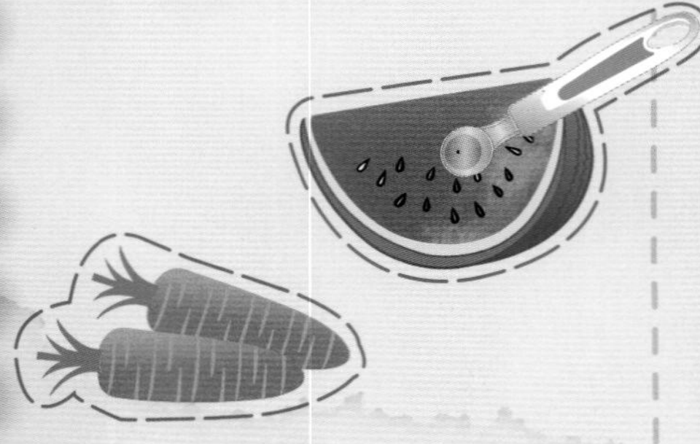

Get Set!

1. Combine the first 7 ingredients in the green mixing bowl. Cover and chill for 15 minutes.
2. In a pinch bowl, combine 2 tablespoons sugar and 2 tablespoons cinnamon.
3. Use the pastry brush to coat one side of each tortilla with melted butter.
4. Sprinkle the tortillas with an even coating of cinnamon and sugar.
5. Cut into wedges using your nylon pizza cutter and arrange in a single layer on the baking sheet.

Get Cooking!

1. Bake the chips for 8–10 minutes. Repeat until all chips are baked.
2. Allow to cool for 15 minutes.
3. Dig in and enjoy with the chilled fruit salsa!

Chicken Quesadillas

SERVES: 2–4

PREP TIME: 20 minutes 

READY TO EAT: 20 minutes 

Get Ready!

Ingredients

- 4 flour tortillas
- ½ lb cheddar cheese
- ¼ lb deli roasted chicken breast slices
- ½ onion
- ½ green pepper
- 2 T oil

Utensils

- frying pan (large)
- cheese grater
- nylon plastic knife
- cookie turner
- pizza cutter
- prep bowl set
- cutting board

Get Set!

1. Chop the onion and green pepper into very thin pieces.
2. Grate the cheese.
3. Chop the chicken into small pieces.

Get Cooking!

1. Heat 1 tablespoon oil in the frying pan over medium-high heat. Add the onions and green pepper pieces. Cook until they soften and the onions turn clear. Remove to a paper towel.
2. Sprinkle half of the cheese on two tortillas. Cover with chicken slices, then top each with half of the sautéed onions and peppers.
3. Sprinkle the remaining cheese over each tortilla and then cover with another tortilla.
4. Heat 1 tablespoon oil in the pan, add the quesadilla and cook over medium-high heat for about 5 minutes per side, or until the tortillas start to brown and the cheese is melted.
5. Cut into wedges using your pizza cutter and dig in and enjoy with chips and salsa!

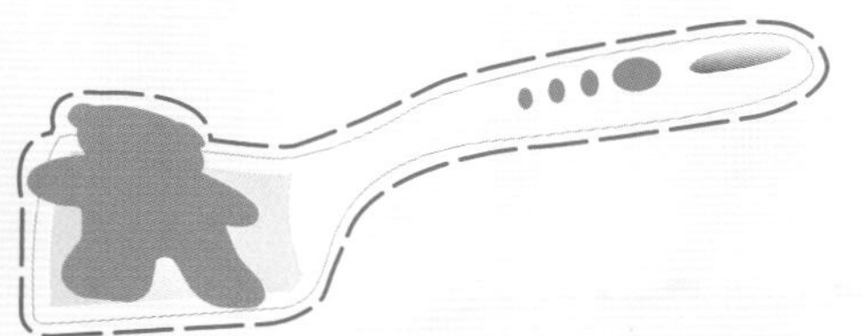

Get Creative!

Quiche Creation

Quiche Lorraine is named after the French city Lorraine. Now it's your turn to create a quiche named after your favorite place. Choose from the ingredients below to create your own unique quiche with its own unique name.

My Quiche is: ______________________

MEAT CHOICES:

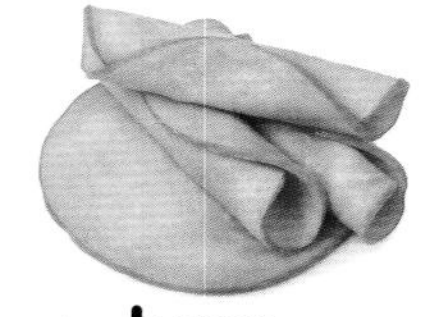
ham

bacon

sausage

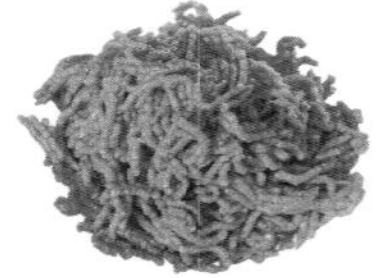
ground beef

shrimp

crab

CHEESE CHOICES:

cheddar cheese

Swiss cheese

feta cheese

goat cheese

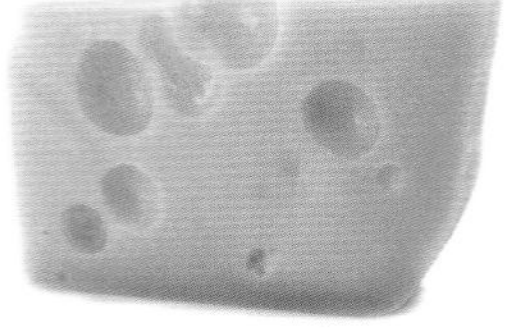
Gruyere cheese

VEGGIE CHOICES:

asparagus

artichoke hearts

tomatoes

broccoli

mushrooms

leeks

potatoes

spinach

Where Am I?

There are 8 words hidden in the puzzle below. Seven of them are common cooking ingredients. Use the clues below to find and circle the 7 ingredients. Then, answer the question below the puzzle to figure out what the 8th word is and find it in the puzzle. [NOTE: Words can be vertical, horizontal, or diagonal.]

I am a breakfast meat that comes from a pig. ____________

I am a breakfast food that comes from a chicken. ____________

I am made from wheat and am used to make bread. ____________

I am made from milk and am used as a pizza topping. ____________

I am a white spice. ____________

I come from a cow and can be churned into butter. ____________

I am a vegetable that can make you cry. ____________

Q	B	N	I	F	C	T	G
N	D	A	L	S	E	L	M
R	F	O	C	S	X	A	S
Z	U	M	E	O	G	S	C
R	Q	E	F	S	N	G	R
C	H	Q	U	I	C	H	E
C	N	O	I	N	O	X	A
I	U	W	X	W	W	R	M

I am a kind of pie you could make with the ingredients in the puzzle. ____________

Have Some Fun! Solutions

RECIPE 1 Oatmeal Carrot Muffins

Rhyme Time (pg. 25)

Get Ready!
section on pages 16–17.

power/flour
flutter/butter
fault/salt
pin/tin
loon/spoon
tease/cheese

Get Set!
section on pages 18–19.

treasure/measure
risk/whisk
trait/grate
cry/dry
legs/eggs
matter/batter

Get Cooking!
section on pages 20–21.

will/fill
cake/bake
rest/test
pool/cool
hole/bowl
lost/frost

RECIPE 2 Fruit Pizza

Odd Ingredient Out (pg. 37)

Fruit	Veggies	Grains	Protein	Dairy
apple	rice	bread	nuts	milk
grapes	broccoli	crackers	cheese	yogurt
chicken	zucchini	pasta	eggs	strawberry
banana	potato	ice cream	lettuce	cheese
strawberry	lettuce	rice	chicken	ice cream

RECIPE 3 Banana Cream Pie

What Am I? (pg. 49)

vanilla
pizza cutter
whipped cream
flour
cherry
Brussels sprouts
rolling pin
whisk
banana
chicken

RECIPE 4 Apple Pie Cake

Fruit and Veggie Rainbow (pg. 61)

carrot (orange)
broccoli (green)
lemon (yellow)
apple (red, yellow, green)
strawberries (red)
eggplant (purple)
corn (yellow)
kiwi (brown and green)
banana (yellow and white)
tomato (red)
grapes (purple, green)

RECIPE 5 Peanut Butter Whoopie Cookies

What's My Nickname (pg. 73)

CLUES:

- ton**g**s
- c**o**lander
- co**o**kie cutter
- **b**owl
- m**e**asuring cup
- **r**olling pin
- whi**s**k

ANSWER: Goobers

RECIPE 7 French Toast Pops

Where Does This Come From? (pg. 97)

strawberry – jam
lemon – lemonade
potato – french fries
corn – tortilla chips
wheat – cereal
milk – cheese
cow – burger
peanuts – peanut butter
chicken – chicken nuggets

RECIPE 6 Italian Meatballs

Crossword Puzzle (pg. 85)

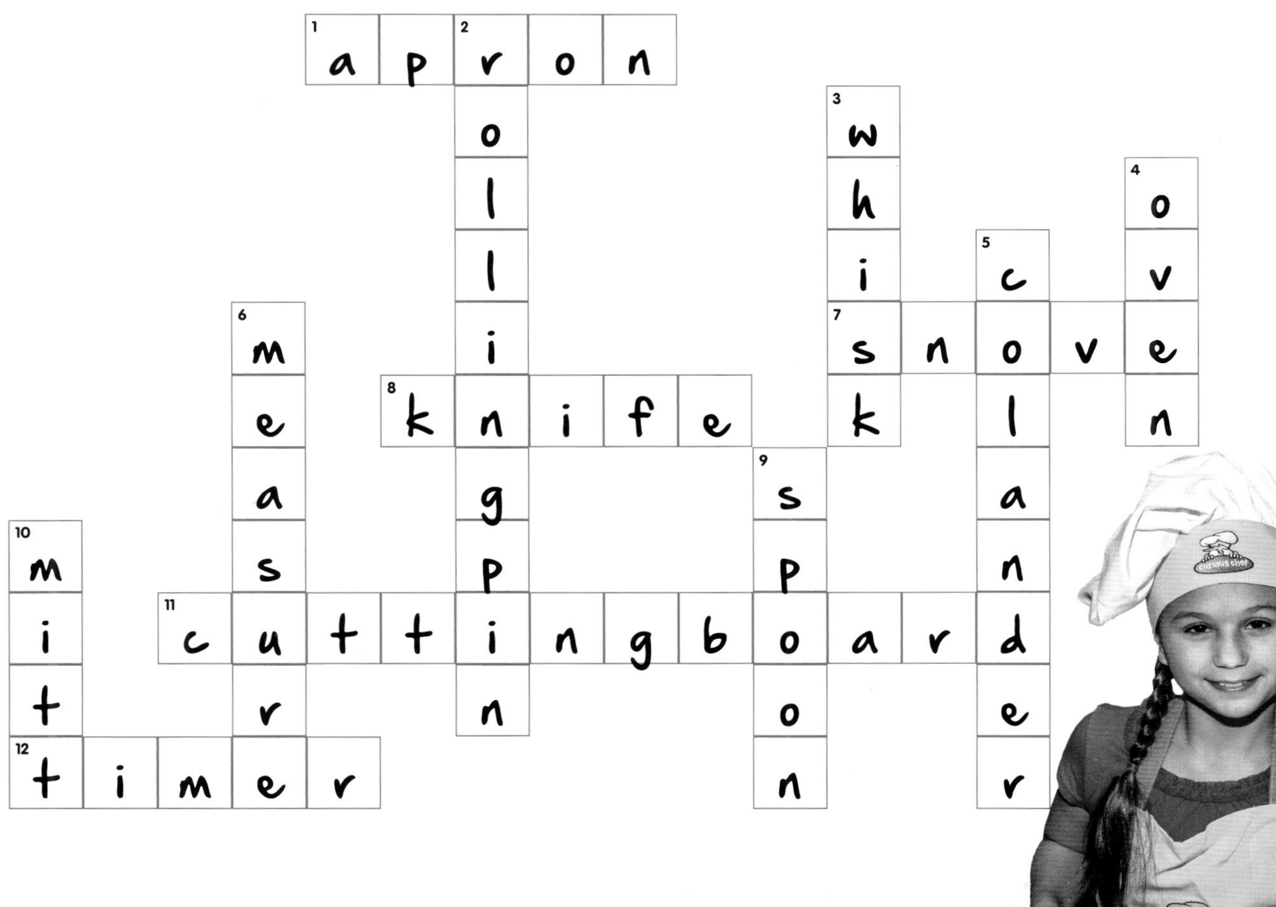

Have Some Fun! Solutions

RECIPE 8 Chocolate Zucchini Muffins

True or False? (pg. 109)

TRUE	FALSE
p	f
r	i
n	s
b	u
l	m
i	l
d	f
t	c
v	n

ANSWER: muffin tin

RECIPE 9 Sausage and Potato Frittata

Food Geography (pg. 121)

oranges/Florida
potatoes/Idaho
peaches/Georgia
cheese/Wisconsin
crab cakes/Maryland
lobster/Maine

pineapples/Hawaii
wheat/Kansas
corn/Iowa
artichokes/California
shrimp/Louisiana
salmon/Alaska

RECIPE 10 Ice Cream Sandwich Cookies

Kitchen Scavenger Hunt (pg. 133)

Answers vary.

RECIPE 11 Baked Peaches 'n Cream

Which One Is Different? (pg. 145)

row 1: egg/e
row 2: apple/a
row 3: cucumber/c
row 4: pineapple/p
row 5: hot dog/h

ANSWER: peach

RECIPE 12 Quiche Lorraine

Where Am I? (pg. 157)

1. bacon
2. egg
3. cheese
4. flour
5. salt
6. cream
7. onion
8. quiche